Essential
Tenerife

by

PAUL MURPHY

Paul Murphy has been a 'professional tourist' for over
eight years, during which time he has written a total of
20 guidebooks and contributed to many more travel
publications. This is his third guidebook covering
the Canary Islands.

Produced by AA Publishing

Written by Paul Murphy
Peace and Quiet section
by Paul Sterry
Original photography by
Rob Moore and Clive Sawyer

Reprinted Apr 1998
First published 1997

Edited, designed and produced
by AA Publishing.
© The Automobile Association
1997
Maps © The Automobile
Association 1997

Distributed in the United Kingdom
by AA Publishing, Norfolk House,
Priestley Road, Basingstoke,
Hampshire, RG24 9NY.

A CIP catalogue record for this
book is available from the British
Library.

ISBN 0 7495 1224 5

The contents of this publication are
believed correct at the time of
printing. Nevertheless, the
publishers cannot be held
responsible for any errors or
omissions, or for changes in
details given in this guide or for
the consequences of any reliance
on the information provided by the
same. Assessments of attractions,
hotels, restaurants and so forth are
based upon the author's own
experience and, therefore,
descriptions given in this guide
necessarily contain an element of
subjective opinion which may not
reflect the publisher's opinion or
dictate a reader's own experience
on another occasion.
We have tried to ensure
accuracy in this guide, but things
do change and we would be
grateful if readers would advise
us of any inaccuracies they may
encounter.

Published by AA Publishing, a
trading name of Automobile
Association Developments
Limited, whose registered office is
Norfolk House, Priestley Road,
Basingstoke, Hampshire,
RG24 9NY.
Registered number 1878835.

Colour separation: BTB Digital
Imaging, Whitchurch, Hampshire.

Printed by: Printers S.R.L., Trento,
Italy.

Front cover picture: *Playa de las
Teresitas, Santa Cruz*

Contents

This book employs a simple rating system to help choose which places to visit:

    'top ten'

◆◆◆ do not miss
◆◆ see if you can
◆ worth seeing if you have time

Introduction and Background

INTRODUCTION

The Canary Islands lie just to the north of the Tropic of Cancer, between 60 and 180 miles (100 and 300km) off the coast of Africa. The islands belong to Spain which is situated around 660 miles (1,100km) to the north. The Canaries were born as an international holiday playground in the late 1950s when Gran Canaria became the place to be seen. However, in recent years the island has taken second place to Tenerife.

Tenerife is by far the largest of the Canary Islands (measuring 794 square miles/2,057sq km). From its eastern to its western extremities it measures around 80 miles (130km) and from Puerto de la Cruz on the north coast to Los Cristianos in the south (via Teide) is around 54 miles (90km).

Tenerife is also the chirpiest of the Canaries with many more things to do and see than the other islands. It has three major resorts: Puerto de la Cruz, which has welcomed visitors for over a century, and two southern newcomers, Los Cristianos and Playa de las Américas. The latter are the brash new face of Tenerife, products of the 1960s and 1970s tourism boom, catering unashamedly for sun'n'fun lovers. Their municipal edges now blur and, combined, this mega-resort attracts many more visitors than the old favourite of Puerto de la Cruz. It is now one of the biggest resorts in Spain. The major advantage they enjoy over Puerto de la Cruz is climate. While the south

*os Gigantes – low-
se apartment,
gh-rise cliffs*

LOCATOR

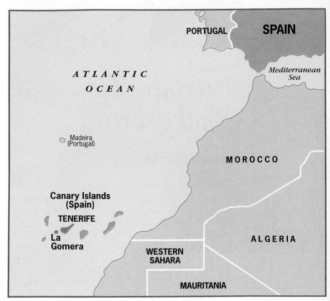

basks in sunshine year round, the north is often overcast, if not wet, for days at a time in winter. This brave new world, and Playa de las Américas in particular, has drawn much criticism for its super-packaged approach. It is enormously popular, however, and not just with the 18 to 30 crowd. Even the most avid supporters of Playa de las Américas would agree that this is not the place to come for an ethnic experience. But if you want two weeks of guaranteed sunshine in well-ordered, cheap, unpretentious, subtropical surroundings, where almost everyone speaks, eats and drinks English, then this is certainly the place to come. By comparison, Puerto de la Cruz – which itself is not without imported bars, fast-food establishments and time-share touts – positively oozes Spanish-colonial character, and this largely accounts for its popularity with a slightly older, more discerning type of holiday-maker. But it is by no means a sleepy place.

The only other significant holiday spot is Los
Gigantes/Puerto de Santiago, a relatively quiet,
largely British enclave on the east coast, though
there are other small resorts in the south.
The resorts are not the place to find the best of
Tenerife. For history and culture you have to go
to the north. Here the fine old colonial towns of
La Laguna, La Orotava, Santa Cruz de Tenerife
(the capital) and Garachico are still virtually
untouched by tourism. For natural scenery
Las Montañas de Anaga (Anaga mountains) in
the northeast and the Teno Massif (Teno Hills)
to the northwest, offer breathtaking panoramas
and wonderful walking trails.

Pico del Teide (Mount Teide), the omnipresent
unofficial island trademark, is the highlight of
Tenerife in every sense. If you only stir once
from your beach towel, do so in its direction.
The volcanic scenery of the Parque Nacional
del Teide is truly out of this world, and many
film crews have used it for science fiction and
dawn-of-time productions.
Partly as a result of the mountain, the weather
contrasts on Tenerife can be startling. In winter
the wind may whistle and snow may drift
around the mountain, while just 25 miles (40km)
south, sunbathers bronze blissfully unaware on
the beach.
The south of the island is hot, dry and arid, with
little natural sightseeing interest though man-
made attractions are improving annually in
terms of quantity and quality. The size of the
island makes it feasible to sightsee in the north
in the morning and sunbathe in the south in the
afternoon. However, distances are exaggerated
by twisting, turning, tiring roads, so you
wouldn't wish to do this every day.
Ironically, given its pre-eminent holiday island
status, the only natural feature that Tenerife is
short on is good beaches. But new beaches are
being built in the south and with alternatives
such as the splendid Lido at Puerto de la Cruz,
the Aguapark Octopus at Playa de las
Américas, few people seem to mind.
For a perfect escape visit the tiny island of
La Gomera. This beautiful spot is the antithesis
of southern Tenerife and will charm anyone
seeking peace, solitude and good old-
fashioned Canarian life in the slow lane.

*Torre del Conde,
La Gomera – a rare
survival from the
Conquest period*

BACKGROUND

Tenerife, like all the Canary Islands, is a
volcanic island, born some 8 to 12 million years
ago, when molten rock and ash forced their
way up from the earth's core to form a cone-
shaped island, scored by *barrancos* (deep
gullies). The islands have been known to
Europe since the dawn of time, but so little
remains of their history prior to the Spanish
Conquest in the 15th century, that even today
the islands' first inhabitants are a mystery.

The Guanches

It would appear that sometime during the 1st to
2nd centuries BC the islands were settled by a
tribe who were tall, fair-skinned, blue-eyed and
blond-haired. They seem to have been of
Berber origin from North Africa (the dark-
skinned Arabs did not colonise North Africa
until much later). The name Guanche derived
from the old Canarian language meaning
'native of Tenerife' but has been adopted as a
generic term for all ancient Canarians.
Despite their relative closeness to Africa, the
islanders remained cut off from the outside

world. However, around the time of Christ, ships from the Roman colony of Mauretania landed on the islands. Legend has it that they found native dogs and thus named the islands *Can-aria* (land of dogs).

The most fascinating aspect of Guanche culture was that, like the Egyptians and the Peruvians, they mummified their dead. They also practised trepanning – the drilling and cutting of holes into the skull. The museum in Santa Cruz has mummies and trepanned skulls.

The Guanches lived in a structured society. The king and his family were the rulers, next in the pecking order came a class of 'nobles', then the rest of the society. The ordinary Guanches were herdsmen and worked the land. They lived mostly in caves (cool in summer, warm in winter), were clothed in goatskins and leather, and their staple food was *gofio* – roasted barley, ground into powder, then mixed with honey and water, and rolled into balls – still produced today. They also fished, using spears tipped with a special substance to stun their prey. Curiously no remains of boats have ever been found, which leaves the unanswered question, how did the Guanches get to the islands from Africa in the first place?

The Conquest

During the 14th century European slave traders and treasure hunters discovered and became the scourge of the islands. They must have been bemused to find a people still living in the Stone Age with no knowledge of metals or even rudimentary technologies.

In 1402 the Norman baron, Jean de Béthencourt, sailed under the flag of Castile (Spain) intending to capture Gran Canaria and Tenerife. Instead he occupied Lanzarote and so began the colonisation of the Canary Islands. The tiny island of El Hierro (at that time the westernmost point in the known world) was the next to fall, but on Tenerife, La Gomera, Gran Canaria and La Palma there was strong resistance from the primitively armed defenders. All of the islands except Tenerife were eventually invaded.

For many years there was an uneasy stand-off between settlers and natives, nowhere more so

Above and right: Two of the island's nine menceys or rulers, romantically portrayed at Candelaria... the sun, long set on the Guanche way of life

than on La Gomera, where the tyrant Hernán Peraza ruled from the Torre del Conde.

In 1478 Ferdinand and Isabella of Spain ordered the second phase of the Conquest to begin. After five years of bitter fighting Gran Canaria was captured and by 1488 La Gomera was also finally subdued.

Four years later La Gomera was visited by Christopher Colombus who used the island as a final staging post before his voyage to the New World. As he was sailing past Tenerife he witnessed a volcanic eruption and noted it in his logbook. Not surprisingly it was taken as an ill omen by his crew.

The following year, 1493, saw the fall of La Palma, leaving Tenerife as the last remaining Guanche outpost.

The Taking of Tenerife

The Spanish came on 1 May 1492, led by Alonso Fernández de Lugo, who landed at the present site of Santa Cruz. There he struck up an alliance with two of Tenerife's nine *menceys* (regional kings) and advanced towards Acentejo (near today's Puerto de la Cruz). His forces were ambushed with the loss of around 900 lives. De Lugo only narrowly escaped by leaving the battlefield disguised as a Guanche. The site today is called La Matanza de Acentejo

(meaning the 'slaughter of Acentejo') and
visible from the motorway is a large mural of a
Guanche blowing a clarion call over the body
of a fallen knight.

De Lugo retreated to Gran Canaria, but
returned late in 1495 to Tenerife and defeated a
confederacy of five Guanche armies close to
La Laguna. The remaining Guanche armies,
already weakened by foreign diseases
(presumably brought over by the Spaniards in
1494), were no match for de Lugo's technically
advanced force and the following year, near the
site of La Matanza de Acentejo, the Spanish
inflicted a crushing revenge. Some estimates
put the number of Guanche casualties as high
as 2,000. The site was proclaimed La Victoria
de Acentejo (victory of Acentejo), in honour of
the last battle of the Conquest and is the name
still borne by the small town here today.

Post-Conquest life varied for the Guanches,
though their numbers were small anyway – on
Tenerife less than 1,000. Many were enslaved,
collaborators were well treated, a minority
intermarried and most were simply ignored by
the new colonists. A significant number
remained in hiding in the mountains. Within a
century or so this ancient society had all but
disappeared.

Post Conquest

It was de Lugo who brought sugar cane to the
island and during the first half of the 16th
century this crop flourished and brought great
wealth to Tenerife. But similar larger plantations
were set up in Brazil and the Antilles, and their
lower unit costs eventually put the Canaries'
sugar trade out of business.

Wine was the next monoculture to bring
prosperity to the island. Already well
established in the eastern islands, the
archipelago's Malvasia (or Canary Wine, as it
was called) was the fashionable drink of
Europe, praised by Shakespeare and enjoyed
in the New World. Tenerife became the largest
producer in the archipelago and was ideally
placed for trade with America. Towns such as
Garachico, La Orotava and, to an extent
La Laguna and Santa Cruz, became rich on the
trade and many of these towns' fine mansions

BACKGROUND

Colonial Architecture

Sturdy stone mansions with carved coats of arms and beautifully crafted wooden balconies, made from the heart of the Canarian pine tree, are the exterior hallmarks of a wealthy merchant's or colonist's home. Inside is a Moorish-style patio, rich with greenery, and perhaps a fountain. Facing onto the courtyard are more balconies. The colonial towns in the north of Tenerife are rich with such architecture.

The Canary pine tree not only helps preserve the water supply but its heart (known as tea*) is used in many a typical balcony*

Nelson Disarmed

In 1797 the growing port of Santa Cruz achieved its most glorious moment. Admiral Nelson had for a long time seen Tenerife as a target and he personally led a bold, surprise attack, leaving his command ship to strike for shore in a rowing boat with two other men. But the Spanish defenders were forewarned and a cannon ball, fired from the cannon *El Tigre* (now on display in the Santa Cruz Museo Militar), shattered the Admiral's arm, killing another man in the boat. A second boat landed but its men were captured. A truce was agreed and the captives were released. The Spanish sent a cask of Canarian wine and best wishes to Nelson for his recovery, while the badly wounded Admiral responded with a gift of English beer and cheese!

date from this period. *Lagars*, huge wooden wine presses, are also reminders of this era. A combination of trade disputes, pricing problems, the War of the Spanish Succession (1701–14) and the rise of Madeira meant that the Malvasia boom was effectively finished by the end of the 17th century. Nonetheless the wine trade continued to be important throughout the 18th century with Tenerife dominant in both production and shipping

Cochineal

During the early part of the 19th century, with the wine trade drying up, cochineal, a red dye extracted from insects which feed on cactus, offered salvation for the eastern Canary islands. Tenerife only partly embraced this industry, realising the potentially harmful environmental effects of replacing large areas of pine forest with cactus. The extraordinarily long needles of Canarian pines on Tenerife absorb water and feed it back into the ground where it eventually soaks down into underground supplies (see either of the two cut-away models of the island's water system at the Bananera in Puerto de la Cruz or the Bananera near Los Cristianos). To have planted large areas of cactus would have jeopardised the island's water supply. The cochineal industry lasted for around 50 years until supplanted by chemical dyes from elsewhere in the world.

Canarian Emigration

Canarians have been travelling to the Americas for centuries: some accompanied Colombus, others went to fight alongside the *conquistadores*. In the late 1700s, with the wine trade in crisis, many emigrated to Venezuela and Cuba where there was a demand for labour. A century or so later the collapse of the cochineal industry provoked another exodus. Today New World links are still manifest: Venezuelan oil is refined in Santa Cruz, Venezuelan rum and *arepas* (see **Food**, page 99) are consumed in bars and there is a daily page on Venezuela in the local papers.

Bananas

In 1852 the Spanish government declared Santa Cruz a free-trade zone, in order to stimulate the faltering Canarian economy, and greatly increased the number of ships landing here. A new monoculture was also developing. Bananas were introduced as a commercial crop in the 1850s to the Valle de la Orotava, where they still thrive. They spread to the north of Tenerife (and to Gran Canaria) and to a lesser extent to La Gomera and La Palma. The British invested heavily in this trade and it flourished from 1881 until World War I. But with the disruption in exports and new competition from bananas from Central America, the islands' economic future was again uncertain.

The 20th Century

In 1912 the Canary Islands were granted self-government (though not independence) from Spain, and 15 years later Santa Cruz de Tenerife became the capital of the western province of the islands, which includes La Gomera, La Palma and El Hierro.

By 1936 war clouds were again looming. Francisco Franco, former commander-in-chief of the Spanish army, was suspected of plotting to overthrow the government and was posted out of the way to Tenerife. In June, however, he met fellow conspirators to confirm the military *coup* which precipitated the Spanish Civil War (1936–9). The islands fell quickly to his forces and within three years General Franco had become dictator of all Spain.

The Canaries were fortunately spared most of the horrific mainland carnage and even prospered economically from the dictatorship. As the rest of Spain went into a protectionist shell, the Canarian free-trade ports assumed greater importance.

The seeds of modern-day tourism were sown in the late 19th century when high-class visitors (mostly British) were attracted to the island by the mild climate and the exotic flora. The first non-stop flight to Tenerife from northern Europe landed in 1959 and during the next two decades the resorts of Los Cristianos and Playa de las Américas were created.

The last few years have been a heady time for Tenerife and the Canary Islands. In 1989 they were accepted as full members of the European Union and have benefitted from grants that have greatly improved the islands' infrastructure. Tourism has continued to boom and in 1995 Tenerife welcomed for the first time, over 4 million visitors.

General Franco – an ill wind for the Canaries?

TENERIFE

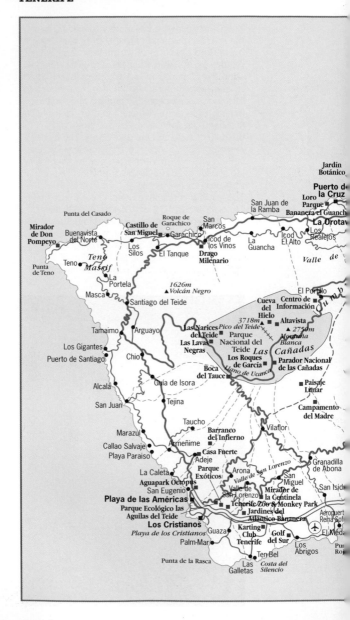

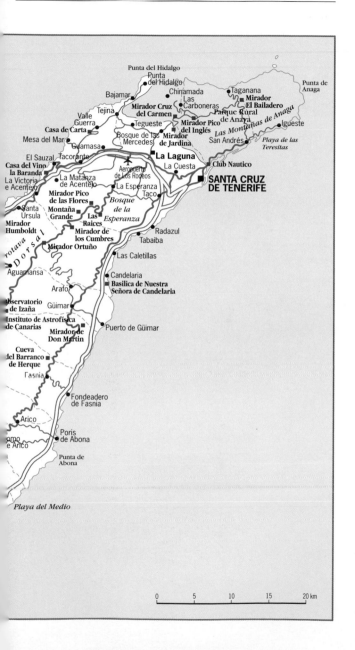

What to See

The Essential rating system:

✓	'top ten'

◆◆◆   do not miss
◆◆   see if you can
◆   worth seeing if you
        have time

SANTA CRUZ DE TENERIFE

Santa Cruz (meaning Holy Cross) takes its name from the cross implanted on the shore by the Spanish *conquistador*, Alonso Fernández de Lugo, in 1494. His compatriot, Sancho de Herrera, had ventured to the place then known as Añaza (or Añazo) 30 years earlier with a small band of men, and with the compliance of the Guanche natives had even built a castle of sorts. Conflicts between locals and newcomers increased and the Spaniards were compelled to leave. By contrast, de Lugo's arrival in 1494 was on a war footing with an army of around 1,000 men. The deep water harbour provided a perfect anchorage and he too built a fort which he used as a bridgehead for his eventual conquest of the whole island. With the final subjugation of the Guanches the city of Santa Cruz was founded in 1496. Thanks to its natural advantages and the growing trade with the Americas, Santa Cruz flourished

The road to the top, a neat straight line through the chaotic moonscape of Mount Teide National Park

as a port and in 1723 it took over the mantle of capital from La Laguna. Its wealth, however, also made it a target for pirates and foreign powers. In 1797 it fought its most illustrious battle, resisting an attack by Admiral Nelson (see box page 13).

By the 19th century Canarian commercial fortunes were waning but in 1852 Santa Cruz received a much needed boost when it was given the status of free port (thus lowering duties and trade barriers) by the Spanish Crown.

Today Santa Cruz is also the administrative centre of the eastern islands and is still an important commercial port, particularly for oil shipments and processing. For holiday visitors it's a busy, though rarely stressful, town and, refreshingly, one of only two conurbations on the island (the other is La Laguna) which do not rely on tourism. It has many grand buildings (as well as a good number of modern eyesores) and in parts a somewhat faded air. Recently the *Cabildo* (island council) has begun to realise the capital's tourist potential and has organised a mini land-train that skirts the main sights. To really appreciate the city, hop aboard the train for a complete circuit then take a leisurely stroll through the heart of Santa Cruz, stopping to admire its museums, to sip a *café con leche* in its tree-shaded plazas, before finishing your walk at the beautiful García Sanabria Park.

SANTA CRUZ DE TENERIFE

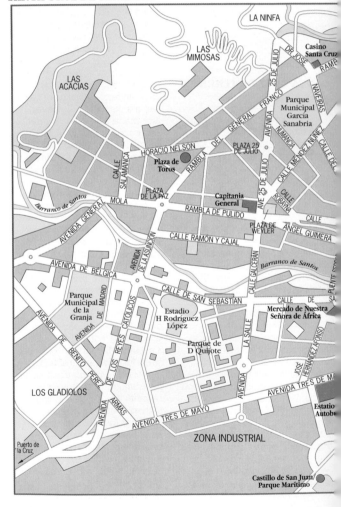

Information on opening times etc has been provided for guidance only. We have tried to ensure accuracy, but things do change and we would advise readers to check locally before planning visits to avoid any possible disappointment.

What to See in Santa Cruz

◆◆

IGLESIA DE NUESTRA SEÑORA DE LA CONCEPCIÓN (CHURCH OF OUR LADY OF THE CONCEPTION)

Plaza de la Iglesia

This handsome landmark church, first built in the early 16th century, is one of the most important historical buildings in Santa Cruz.

It used to house the British flag captured during Nelson's abortive raid (see page 13) and also the original cross carried by de Lugo in 1494 (see page 19). Unfortunately the church became so dilapidated that it has been closed for several years and long-term restoration work is under way and is scheduled to continue until 1999. Whether the cross and flag will return here is not known but the tomb of General Gutiérrez, Nelson's foe in 1797, is a permanent fixture.

On the same plaza look out for the fine façade of the **Tinerfeña Fábrica de Tabacos** (Tenerife Tobacco Factory), which dates from 1880.

◆

IGLESIA DE SAN FRANCISCO (CHURCH OF ST FRANCIS)

Plaza del Príncipe

Formerly the monastery church of San Pedro de Alcántara, this atmospheric building dates from around 1680. Its elaborately decorated interior is notable for a painted arch, some splendid baroque 18th-century *retablos* (retables) and, in the chapel to the right of the main altar, a fine *mudéjar* (Moorish) ceiling.

◆◆
MERCADO DE NUESTRA SEÑORA DE ÁFRICA (MARKET OF OUR LADY OF AFRICA)

Calle de San Sebastián
This bustling, covered market is as colourful as its name suggests, selling fruit, vegetables, flowers, fish and meat. On Sundays a lively *rastro* (flea market) is held next to the halls, where you can pick up leatherware and craft items, plus all manner of odds and ends.
Open: main market: Monday to Saturday 09.00–13.00hrs; *rastro*: Sunday 10.00–14.00hrs.

◆
MUSEO MILITAR (MILITARY MUSEUM)

Calle San Isidro (tel: 27 16 62)
The most notable exhibit in this collection of hardware and regalia is *El Tigre* (the Tiger),

El Tigre – *'the tiger' which savaged Admiral Nelson in 1797*

the cannon which is said to have fired the shot which shattered Admiral Nelson's right arm at the Battle of Santa Cruz in 1797.
Open: Tuesday to Sunday 09.30–13.30hrs.

◆◆
MUSEO MUNICIPAL DE BELLAS ARTES (CITY MUSEUM OF FINE ARTS)

Calle José Murphy (tel: 24 43 58)
The exterior of this imposing building is lined with busts of Canarian musicians, poets and philosophers. It is the home of the island's finest art collection, with many Spanish paintings and sculptures on loan from the Prado in Madrid, and an important collection of 17th- to 19th-century Canarian paintings. Among several historic scenes is the momentous landing of de Lugo in 1494 (see **Background**, page 10). Contemporary works from the archipelago are also on display here.

On the corner next to the museum is the **Círculo de Amistad XII de Enero**, the former home of a recreational society (akin to a gentlemen's club), founded in 1903, the same date as the building, which is now a cultural centre. This is one of the city's most glorious structures, recently renovated, and a pastiche of many styles. It is best viewed from the raised **Plaza del Príncipe**, a real jungle of a square with giant Indian Laurel trees shading a bandstand.
Open: museum: Monday to Friday 10.00–19.45hrs.

◆
MUSEO DE LA NATURALEZA Y EL HOMBRE (MUSEUM OF NATURE AND MANKIND)
Calle Fuentes Morales (tel: 21 30 00)
The former Museum of Archaeology, with its impressive collection of Guanche skulls, bones and mummified specimens, is being slowly moved to its new home in the Antiguo Hospital Civil (old city hospital), which it will share with

Doing it in tiles – decorative bench detail at Plaza 25 de Julio

displays on Canarian flora and fauna. In the interim a series of temporary exhibitions is being staged. Captions are only written in Spanish.
Open: Tuesday to Sunday 10.00–20.00hrs.

◆◆
PARQUE MUNICIPAL GARCÍA SANABRIA (GARCÍA SANABRIA PARK)
This beautifully laid out mature park, designed in the 1920s, is a fine place to take a rest from shopping and to escape the city bustle. In the midst of the exotic trees and shrubs there are fountains, statuary, modern sculpture and a famous floral clock, alongside which is a good café.
En route to the park from the centre are two delightful plazas. **Plaza de Weyler** is a popular flower-filled garden square with a lovely marble fountain. By contrast **Plaza 25 de Julio** is a small round circle with an unusual fountain of eight green

glazed frogs spouting water. Around it are a number of benches, beautifully decorated with colourful *azulejos* (ceramic tiles). These were produced in Seville in the 1920s and some of them carry picturesque advertising messages.

◆◆
PARQUE MARÍTIMO (CÉSAR MANRIQUE)

Castillo de San Juan (tel: 20 32 44); drive or walk along the coast road from the Avenida de José Antonio Primo de Rivera

Incongruously tucked away in the industrial dockyard area, the Parque Marítimo is the city's most ambitious ever leisure project. Based around the old Castillo de San Juan (Castle of St John) it is proposed that this will eventually include a cultural centre, a maritime museum, a folk museum, an exhibition centre and various other leisure facilities, all built and landscaped to the specifications and strict Canarian environmental standards laid down by the late, great Lanzarote architect César Manrique (see page 50). At the time of writing an excellent seawater lido has been constructed, along the lines of Manrique's famous Lido Martiánez in Puerto de la Cruz (see pages 49–50).
Open: daily, 10.00–18.00hrs.

◆◆
PLAZA DE LA CANDELARIA

This is the main city square, where shoppers and coach parties begin their exploration of Santa Cruz and where itinerant embroidery saleswomen accost potential customers.

At the centre of the square is the statue **El Triunfo de la Candelaria** illustrating the triumph of the Virgin of Candelaria in converting to Christianity the four figures below her who represent Guanche chieftains (see **Candelaria**, pages 25–7). The statue is often incorrectly attributed to the Italian sculptor Antonio Canova, but it was probably executed by the Genoese artist, Pasquale Bocciardo, in 1773.

At No 9 on the plaza, behind a dull grey basalt exterior, the Banco Español de Credito now occupies the gracious **Palacio de Carta**, built in 1742. The banking hall is situated in a perfect example of a gleaming darkwood Canarian patio (*open*: during banking hours).

The Virgin triumphant, 'bringer of light' to the Guanche heathens

◆
PLAZA DE ESPAÑA

The rather drab, towering mirrored cross (**Monumento de los Caídos**), which stands in this square and marks the hub of Santa Cruz, is a monument to the dead of the Spanish Civil War (1936–9).

Also on the square are two other huge grey examples of Fascist architecture: the **Palacio Insular** (island government offices) which also houses the tourist information centre and the **Correos** (main post office). It's worth a look inside the foyer of the Palacio Insular (*open*: office hours) to see its fine stained-glass window which features typical scenes of Tenerife.

Excursion from Santa Cruz

◆
CANDELARIA

10 miles (17km) south of Santa Cruz

Candelaria is the island's main point of pilgrimage and its history is a curious and unique mix of shared Guanche and *conquistador* worship. According to legend, in 1392, over a century before the Spanish forces set foot on Tenerife, two Guanches found a figure of the Virgin and Child in a cave on the coast. What happens next varies according to who tells the story.

Plaza de España – the imposing symbol of Santa Crus

The Madonna in full glory in the Basilica de la Candelaria

Some say one of the Guanches accidentally cut his finger on his knife but when he touched the figure it miraculously healed. Another story relates how the Guanches initially tried to throw stones at the figure but were prevented from doing so by an unexplained paralysis of their arms. Whatever really happened the Guanches began to worship the figure and did so until the coming of the Spanish. The local *mencey* (king) chose to side with the newcomers rather than fight against them and so the Spanish attributed the figure with converting the local people to Christianity. It was probably at this time that it was given its name, Candelaria, meaning 'bringer of light'. Subsequently the **Virgen de la Candelaria** has been adopted as the patron saint of all the Canary Islands and on 14 and 15 August each year tens of thousands of Canarian pilgrims converge on the town. Today Candelaria is famous for its huge **Basílica de Nuestra Señora de la Candelaria** and the nine Guanche statues which stand, somewhat forlornly, on the adjacent seafront. These idealised figures represent the nine former *menceys* of Tenerife whose names at least are still perpetuated in today's place names. The basilica dates from 1958 and despite its exterior bulk is unexceptional apart from the famous figure. The original Virgin was lost in a tidal wave in 1826 and the present figure was carved in 1830.

Accommodation

Santa Cruz has no history of tourism and, with Puerto de la Cruz so close, few travellers stay here. If expense is no problem the 5-star **Hotel Mencey**, Dr José Naveiras 38 (tel: 27 67 00), opposite the Parque Municipal García Sanabria is one of the finest hotels in the archipelago, built in grand colonial style with typical Canarian woodwork, gleaming marble, and many fine works of art. Less well-heeled visitors might like to try the 2-star **Atlántico**, Calle del Castillo 12 (tel: 24 63 75) or the 3-star **Plaza** on Plaza de la Candelaria (tel: 27 24 53).

Children

Santa Cruz isn't built for children, but teenagers will no doubt enjoy the somewhat gruesome mummified Guanches at the **Museo de la Naturaleza y El Hombre** while younger children are best taken to the **Parque García Sanabria** which has a children's playground. A splash in the **Parque Marítimo** might be fun but a trip to **Playa de las Teresitas**, 4 miles (6km) from town (see page 38), is probably the best bet of all.

Culture, Entertainment and Nightlife

The **Teatro Guimerá** on Plaza Isla de la Madera is the city's principal venue for classical concerts, opera, theatre (Spanish-language only) and ballet performances. The Tenerife Symphony Orchestra (TSO) play here regularly during the winter. For information and tickets contact the Cabildo Insular (tel: 60 58 01).

Next door to the theatre, in a former market hall, is the **Centro de Fotografía** (Photography Centre) where temporary exhibitions are staged (*open*: Tuesday to Saturday 10.00–13.00hrs and 17.00–20.00hrs).

Santa Cruz also has a lively nightlife, though it caters almost entirely to locals and Spanish youth. For those brave enough to go native, **KU** on the Avenida de Madrid (tel: 20 36 36) is reckoned to be one of the best discos on the island, if not the archipelago. Rock concerts are held in the **Plaza de Toros** (bull ring) on the Rambla del General Franco.

If you want to gamble the night away playing blackjack, roulette or the slot machines, then the Hotel Mencey (see above) has

Bargain hunting in the Calle del Castillo is a popular morning off from the beach

the **Casino Santa Cruz** (*open*: 20.00–03.00hrs; tel: 29 07 40).

Restaurants
The capital is not noted for tourist restaurants, with the most highly rated eating establishments (catering for

Carnival Crazy
In 1987 the world's biggest carnival ball took place in Santa Cruz. According to figures ratified by the *Guinness Book of Records* over 240,000 revellers packed the Plaza de España to celebrate the last night of the festivities which are held annually in the run-up to Lent.

locals and the business community), along or just off the Rambla del General Franco and the Calle de Méndez Nuñez. Off the former at Calle General Goded 13 is the prestigious **El Coto de Antonio** (tel: 27 21 05). At No 17 is the more affordable **Los Troncos** (tel: 28 41 52) serving Canarian and Basque specialities.

On the small streets around the main central area there is no shortage of local bars and small restaurants serving *tapas* and local food. The prominent **Cafetería Olympo** (tel: 24 17 38) on Plaza de Candelaria, may show every sign of being a tourist trap, but the food, and views from here, can be good.

If fish is your dish, then it is worth travelling the short distance (5 miles/8km) to San Andrés where there is a clutch of top-quality fish and seafood restaurants.

Shopping

Santa Cruz is sold by most tour operators primarily as a shopping trip. Yet, while there certainly is a large number of shops here, quality, prices and the range of goods are not exceptional. The prime area is on and around Calle del Castillo, the street leading off from the Plaza de la Candelaria. A notable feature are the Asian-owned *bazaars* which are some of the few places on the island where you can try your hand at price negotiating.

The best shopping experience is without doubt the **Mercado de Nuestra Señora de África** (see page 22).

Special Events

The great event in the Santa Cruz calendar is *Carnaval* (see box, page 28). Centring on the Plaza de España, the festivities are launched here before spreading to the rest of the island. Huge amounts of money are spent on extravagant stage sets which open out to reveal the carnival queen and princesses in all their glory, and the ensuing celebrations are said to be the biggest outside Río de Janeiro. Special coaches run from all over the island and the event is also televised.

Sport

CD Tenerife, the island's football team, play in the Spanish First Division in Santa Cruz (see **Sport**, page 111).

Fishy business. Perfect if you are self-catering, or just fun to look

THE NORTHEAST

The northeast corner of the island is a highlight of many a Tenerife trip, yet despite its great beauty, the best beach on Tenerife, two of the island's best museums and one of its most handsome and historic cities, the region is still relatively unexplored. For independent travellers this in itself is a major part of its appeal and this corner of the island is a world away from the fleshpots of the packaged south.

◆
BAJAMAR
18 miles (30km) northeast of Puerto de la Cruz
Bajamar is one of the oldest tourist resorts on the island and has a rather tired, dated look. It is still quite popular, mainly with elderly German visitors, seeking peace and quiet. There is no town or village centre here

The magnificent, unspoiled greenery of the Anaga

and swimmers must choose between a small black beach or seawater pools by the promenade.
Punta del Hidalgo, 5 miles (3km) to the north, is its newer sister resort with many of its hotels enjoying excellent cliff-top positions. There are fine views from the point itself and the views of sunsets from here are probably the best on Tenerife.

◆◆◆
CASA DE CARTA MUSEO ETNOGRÁFICO DE TENERIFE (MUSEUM OF ETHNOGRAPHY)
15 miles (25km) northeast of Puerto de la Cruz, Tacoronte to Valle Guerra Road (tel: 54 30 53)
This beautiful house, built in the late 17th to early 18th century, is home to the finest ethnographic

collection in the archipelago. The building itself is a superlative example of Canarian architecture with an outstanding display of porticos, patios and richly carved woodwork, rarely found nowadays under one single roof. It takes its name from the Carta family who lived here for several generations, administering the land rights of the region.

The most colourful exhibits are the traditional Canarian costumes, which date from the 18th century to the present day. You can see how these were made in the weaving and needlework rooms and how different regions and islands have their own styles and colours for daily wear and for holidays. Other displays include reconstructions of various rooms, a ceramics collection, and cereal and *gofio*-related (see **Food and Drink**, page 100) exhibits.

Open: Tuesday to Sunday 10.00–20.00hrs.

◆◆
CASA DEL VINO LA BARANDA (THE BARANDA HOUSE OF WINE)

just off the Autopista del Norte, El Sauzal (km21) exit, 11 miles (18km) east of Puerto de la Cruz (tel: 57 25 35)

This enterprising new visitor attraction, housed in a 17th-century farmhouse, is a first-class introduction to the wines of Tenerife. A ten-minute video explains the history of winemaking on the island and underlines its recent renaissance. A small museum complements the video (English notes available), and then it is on to the all-important tasting room, where for a modest charge you can sample up to 10 of the 150 island wines which are showcased here. There is a good restaurant on site (tel: 56 33 88) and the coastal views are excellent.

Open: Tuesday to Saturday 11.00–20.00hrs; Sunday and holidays 11.00–18.00hrs.

###
CHINAMADA

Hidden deep in the heart of the Anaga mountains, until 1993 Chinamada had no roads and its cave-dwelling inhabitants had an hour's walk to Las Carboneras. Now a dirt track road links the two villages, though (at the time of writing) it is still very bumpy and walking is the most comfortable option. *En route*, note the green-velvet peak of **Roque de Taborno**, away to your right. This rises to 2,319 feet (707m) and has a distinctive bullet-shaped basalt peak. As you approach the village you will see the first cave houses straight ahead. Follow the track, which wiggles to the left through a tiny pass. The **view** to the left, across the deep green ravine of Barranco de Tomadero is stunning. Listen and you will probably hear bells. Goats graze on these seemingly impossibly steep terraced slopes, providing meat and cheese for the 30 or so people of Chinamada. Their houses are small and are cut back into the rocky ridge but inside the furnishings and facilities are far from Stone Age. You can walk along the narrow path alongside the houses and if you are feeling inspired by the scenery it's around an hour's walk all the way down to Punta del Hidalgo (from where buses run back to La Laguna).

◆◆◆ LA LAGUNA ✓

La Laguna was founded in 1496 by the island's conqueror, Alonso Fernández de Lugo, who established it as capital of all the Canaries (the lagoon after which it was named has long since gone). La Laguna remained the island's principal city until the early 18th century and its numerous handsome 16th- and 17th-century mansions attest to the wealth of this era. Yet despite its wonderful architecture and its authentic Spanish atmosphere, it is untouched by tourism. Today it is the most important town on the island after Santa Cruz and its university – the oldest in the archipelago, originally founded in 1701 (though the present institution began in 1817) –

ensures that during term time it has a youthful air.

There is no proper tourist office in La Laguna. The *ayuntamiento* (town hall) claims an *oficina de turismo* but it is well hidden down long corridors and the information is rudimentary, though they can supply a city map (try also the Hotel Apartments Nivaria, on Plaza del Adelentado). Fortunately most of the main points of interest are restricted to a small area. Start in the **Plaza del Adelantado**, with its white marble fountain, walk up **Calle Obispo Rey Redondo**, turn right into Los Bolos to the **Plaza Junta Suprema** (a small triangular shaped plaza featuring a curious standing stone) then walk back down **Calle San Agustín** which runs parallel to Obispo Rey Redondo. It's best to visit in the morning and imperative to avoid the *siesta* when La Laguna becomes a ghost town.

Plaza del Adelantado – a shady place to sit and watch traditional island town life

What to See in La Laguna

◆
AYUNTAMIENTO (TOWN HALL)
Calle Obispo Rey Redondo
The town hall was originally built in the 16th century but rebuilt and restored in typical Canarian style in 1822. Upstairs is splendid wooden panelling and a Moorish-style wooden oriel window.
Adjoining the town hall is the **Casa de los Capitanes Generales** (House of the Captain Generals). This splendid former residence of the island's field marshals was built 1624–31 and is now used for temporary exhibitions (closed at other times).
Open: town hall: during office hours; Casa de los Capitanes Generales: Monday 17.00–20.00hrs; Tuesday to Saturday 11.00–13.00hrs and 17.00–20.00hrs; Sunday 11.00–13.00hrs.

◆
CATEDRAL (CATHEDRAL)
Calle Obispo Rey Redondo
This huge church was founded in 1515 although its façade dates from 1820 and the interior was remodelled in 1904–5. Despite its hemmed in position the front is very attractive with palm trees and a charming duck pond which even has a period-style duck house! By contrast the interior is dark and cavernous and its treasures are not immediately apparent. The tabernacle on the high altar is the work of Luján Pérez, one of the greatest Canarian wood sculptors. To the right of here,

note the glowing gilded baroque *retablo* in the Capilla de la Virgen de los Remedios (Chapel of the Virgin of Remedies). By contrast, also to the right (and slightly behind) the high altar, is the very plain, surprisingly understated tomb of the city founder, Don Alonso Fernández de Lugo, *Conquistador de la Tenerife y La Palma* (Conqueror of Tenerife and La Palma), buried here in 1525.
Open: Monday to Saturday 08.00–13.30hrs and 17.00–19.30hrs; Sunday, services only.

◆◆◆
IGLESIA DE NUESTRA SEÑORA DE LA CONCEPCIÓN (CHURCH OF OUR LADY OF THE CONCEPTION)
Calle Obispo Rey Redondo
This splendid triple-naved church is the oldest in La Laguna, begun in 1502, but rebuilt over the centuries and presenting a mix of Gothic, Renaissance and baroque styles. The landmark seven-storey tower dates from the 17th century but has Moorish features. Within is the richest interior on the island. There is a small admission charge but this includes an excellent guide leaflet (in Spanish) which details all the points of interest. Outstanding among these are the 16th-century multi-coloured coffered **ceiling panels** and the flamboyant 18th-century cedarwood **pulpit**. Together these constitute some of the finest craftsmanship to be found in the whole archipelago. Other noteworthy points are the

The Church of Our Lady of the Immaculate Conception has been declared a national shrine

Canarian Churches

There are many fine churches on the island which reflect Spanish colonial-style architecture. Their most distinctive feature is the *mudéjar* (Moorish-influenced) coffered ceiling panels. These ornamental concave panels are beautifully crafted, carved and also sometimes colourfully painted.

The other point to note are the *retablos*, the highly ornamental screen-like structures around the altars, of which there may be many.

many fine *retablos* (some dating back to the 17th century), the gleaming silver-plated **Capilla del Santísimo** and the **Baptisterio** (baptistery). In the latter are two huge fonts. The large glazed 16th-century font came from Seville and is said to have been used to baptise Guanche leaders.

Open: Monday to Friday 10.00hrs–noon; Saturday and Sunday, services only.

◆

INSTITUTO DE CANARIAS CABRERA PINTO (CABRERA PINTO INSTITUTE OF CANARIAN STUDIES)

This study institute, housed in a former Augustinian convent, is renowned for one of the most beautiful patios in the Canaries. Unfortunately it is presently closed for long-term renovation but its handsome bell tower is still a fine sight.

Adjacent is the impressive shell of the 17th-century **Monasterio de San Agustín** (Monastery of St Augustine), destroyed by fire early this century (no entry). Opposite, notice the charming old-fashioned frontage of the **Imprenta Sigu** bookshop, with a huge thermometer, and reliefs of books, a globe and literary faces.

◆

MONUMENTO JOSÉ DE ANCHIETA (MONUMENT TO JOSÉ DE ANCHIETA)

just outside the town centre, on the roundabout directly off the Autopista del Norte

Father José de Anchieta was born in La Laguna in 1533 on the Plaza del Adelentado. He was the first Christian missionary to Brazil and it is claimed that he converted millions of Brazilian Indians to Christianity. He was also instrumental in founding the city of São Paolo. The statue was a present from the Brazilian government in 1959.

◆◆
MUSEO DE LA CIENCIA Y EL COSMOS (MUSEUM OF SCIENCE AND THE COSMOS)
Vía Láctea, off the La Cuesta road to Santa Cruz (tel: 26 34 54/94)
This entertaining hands-on museum features 70 modules which attempt to explain the workings of the sun, the earth, the universe and the human body. You can listen to sounds from the womb, take a lie detector test, cross a maze of mirrors, see your own skeleton pedalling a bicycle, and much more.
Open: Tuesday to Sunday 10.00–20.00hrs

◆◆◆
MUSEO DE HISTORIA DE TENERIFE
Calle San Agustín 22 (tel: 63 01 03/21)
This is without doubt the best historical museum on Tenerife and charts the history of the island from the 15th century to the present day, with a series of well displayed exhibits. Captions are in Spanish but an English guide and leaflet are available.
The museum is housed in the Casa Lercaro, a former nobleman's mansion begun in 1593. This in itself is a star attraction and is one of the most impressive colonial-style houses open to the public in all the Canaries.
Open: Tuesday to Saturday 10.00–17.00hrs; Sunday 10.00–14.00hrs.

The history of Tenerife fishing as presented by the Museo de Historia de Tenerife

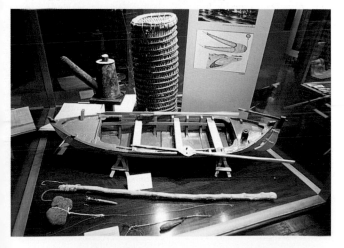

◆◆
PALACIO EPISCOPAL (BISHOP'S PALACE)
Calle San Agustín
Only the beautiful patio of this 17th-century palace is open to the public but it is well worth stepping inside. Note too the fine baroque façade. Opposite is the beautiful doorway of No 23, formerly part of the original **University** (Universidad de San Fernando).
Open: Palacio Episcopal: daily, 09.00–13.00hrs and 16.00–18.00hrs; University library: Monday to Friday 16.30–18.30hrs.

◆◆◆
PLAZA DEL ADELANTADO
This bustling shady square is the focal point of La Laguna and also features the best architectural ensemble on the island. To the right of the *ayuntamiento* (see page 33) is the **Iglesia Convento Santa Catalina** (Convent Church of Saint Catalina) topped by an unusual lattice-work gallery. The interior is notable for its fine baroque *retablos* and its silver-plated **high altar**. A little way along Calle Dean Palahi, to the right of the church, is a side entrance. On the other side of the small courtyard note the door with a revolving cradle compartment. This was used by mothers who wished to abandon their children to the convent anonymously.
Adjacent to the Convento is the **Palacio de Nava**, a forbidding grey colonial baroque palace, begun in 1585. On the opposite side of the square the lively

Mercado Municipal (municipal market) also has a latticed gallery. Next door is the charming tiny yellow-washed **Ermita de San Miguel** (St Michael's Hermitage), built in 1507 by order of de Lugo. It is now an exhibition hall.
Open: Church of Santa Catalina: Monday to Saturday 09.00–12.30hrs and 16.00–18.00hrs; Sunday 10.00hrs–noon and 16.00–18.00hrs; Ermita de San Miguel: Monday 17.00–20.00hrs; Tuesday to Saturday 11.00–13.00hrs and 17.00–20.00hrs; Sunday 11.00–13.00hrs.

Best of the Rest
In addition to the sights highlighted here are many more interesting buildings in the old centre of La Laguna. Calle San Agustín is a particularly handsome street with several reminders of the Colonial period. Opposite the Palacio Episcopal (see above) notice the doorway of No 23. Now an economic institute, this was once the entrance to the original University. No 16, the **Consejo Consultivo de Canarias,** features yet another perfect Canarian patio in a 1746 house.
On Calle Obispo Rey Redondo the **Teatro Leal** is a large pink and yellow theatre with two bright-red cupolas, dating from 1915. Near the top of this street is the charming **Plaza de la Concepción** where fine houses look onto a square with two dragon trees and a bizarre art nouveau structure which covers an electricity sub-station.

◆◆◆
LAS MONTAÑAS DE ANAGA (ANAGA MOUNTAINS) ✓

The panoramic, green-cloaked Anaga mountain region is an excellent area for walking, and recent initiatives (more signposting, maps and routes, and a new information centre) make this an easier option than ever before. The Anaga is also a superb area to tour by car with several *miradores* (viewpoints) guaranteeing a memorable trip as long as the weather is fine. If the clouds are low (as they often are in this region) then leave it for another day.

The Anaga are extremely steep, though rising to only 3,360 feet (1,024m) their peaks are modest. The best way to explore the mountains is simply to follow the signs from La Laguna.

The first viewing point is the **Mirador de Jardina**, with a view as the name suggests, right into the back garden of La Laguna. Next, at an elevation of 3,018 feet (920m) is the **Mirador**

Cruz del Carmen with a similar but much wider perspective, taking in both coasts. A new visitor centre here showcases the Anaga Rural Park (as the area has recently been designated) with a video and information panels, as well as leaflets and information on walks. Adjacent is a restaurant and a 17th-century chapel holding the venerated figure of Nuestra Señora de las Mercedes.

At a height of 3,254 feet (992m) the **Mirador Pico del Inglés** is the loftiest of all the Anaga viewing points. It offers one of the finest panoramas in the whole archipelago and reveals the Anaga mountains in all their glory. On a clear day you may even see Gran Canaria. One explanation for its name ('Peak of the English') is that in the days of Raleigh and Hawkins, English spies sent signals from here, to their marauding ships down

Peak of delight – the view from Mirador de Jardina

below, whenever a Spanish galleon was sighted.

Finally, at El Bailadero is the **Mirador Taganana** which gives a bird's-eye view over the pretty white village of Taganana, strung out along a knife-edge of rock, which plunges steeply towards the coast.

PLAYA DE LAS TERESITAS

6 miles (9km) northeast of Santa Cruz

This beautiful beach is the finest on the island, created in the early 1970s from some four million sackfuls of sand imported from the Sahara. It curves around in a long golden crescent with safe shallow waters, thanks to a man-made reef which also helps to keep the precious sand from being washed away. A small fishing fleet lies at anchor at San Andrés while the other end is protected by tall cliffs. A backdrop of mountains and palm trees completes the picture-postcard scene. The beach is well maintained, rarely very busy (except at summer weekends and holidays when

---

Bosque de las Mercedes

The Bosque de las Mercedes ('Wood of Our Lady of Mercies') is a dense, primeval, subtropical laurel forest, made up of around 20 different tree species. This sort of vegetation, also found on La Gomera (see pages 84–93), is now rare and much prized by botanists and ecologists. The wood begins around 2½ miles (4km) north from La Laguna and stretches to the mountains.

---

local people flock here) and is unspoilt by any surrounding developments. There are pedaloes for hire but there are no other watersports' facilities for rent here.

The adjacent village of San Andrés is renowned for its fish restaurants. Notice too its ruined castle, which was smashed cleanly in half by a flood tide some 30 years ago.

For a splendid view of the beach continue on the road towards the picturesque village of Igueste, to a group of derelict buildings where you can pull safely off the road. On the other side of this small headland you can peer down to the small black-sand beach of **Las Gaviotas**, which is popular with nudists.

EL SAUZAL

10 miles (16km) northeast of Puerto de la Cruz

Much money has recently been spent on upgrading the small town of El Sauzal and the results are impressive. The **Mirador de la Garañona** offers a simply breathtaking view of the north coast cliffs which drop sheer some 300–400 feet (100–130m) from here. There is a pleasant café from which to admire the view and landscaped gardens. In the centre the 16th-century **Iglesia de San Pedro** (Church of St Peter) is a handsome building with a white Moorish-style dome. The adjacent **town hall** is built in typical Canarian style and features beautiful gardens on steep terraces with a cascading waterfall.

Close by is the Casa del Vino La Baranda (see page 31).

Glorious, golden Saharan sand awaits Las Teresitas sunbathers

◆◆
TACORONTE
12½ miles (20km) northeast of Puerto de la Cruz

This straggling town is famous for its wine and its two churches, both signposted below the busy main centre. **Iglesia del Cristo de los Dolores** (Church of Christ of the Sorrows) is a dark-stone former monastic church famous for its much-venerated 17th-century figure of Christ, who does indeed look full of sorrows, with graphically depicted wounds. Notice too the coloured coffered ceiling panels. Further down the hill is the handsome **Iglesia de Santa Catalina**, built in 1664, its tall grey and white tower a landmark. It has a beautiful interior with some splendid coloured woodwork, some of the most impressive large *retablos* on Tenerife and superb coffered ceiling panels. On the way back up to the centre (on the Bajamar road) is a huge and ancient dragon tree, carefully propped up with iron supports.

Tacoronte is the most intensively cultivated vine growing area on Tenerife and one of the best places to sample the fruits of this labour is at the **Bodegas Alvaro**, the largest wine merchant on the island which has two whole floors devoted to the sale of Canarian wines. It is located about a mile or so (2km) from Tacoronte on the road to La Laguna.

Turismo Rural

If you would like to experience Canarian rural life in a rented country house, contact the ATREA office, Carretera Tacoronte-Tejina, 38350 Tenerife (tel: 57 00 15). They offer a small number of properties in and around Tacoronte and El Sauzal, from a 16th-century manor house (from around 9,000 ptas per day) to wooden chalets on the cliffs (at around 2,000 ptas per day). ATREA also offer horse riding near Tacoronte.

THE NORTHEAST

Accommodation

There are few hotels in this region and most visitors tend to be based in Puerto de la Cruz. The best option in La Laguna is the attractive 3-star **Hotel Apartments Nivaria**, on Plaza del Adelantado, tel: 26 42 98. (See also **Turismo Rural** box, page 39.)

Culture, Entertainment and Nightlife

The performing arts are well represented in La Laguna. Ask at the town hall for a copy of the monthly *Agenda Cultural* leaflet which details municipal concerts and exhibitions. The La Laguna Classical Orchestra play at the university and for other events here (and elsewhere in La Laguna) look in the local press. El Sauzal has a small **auditorium** where musical events are staged and which is also the home of the Tenerife English Speaking Theatrical Association (ESTA), tel: 37 12 97.

The popular excursion night out, **Fiesta Canaria Carnaval/ Barbacoa Tacoronte**, is held on Calle Las Toscas (by the Iglesia de Santa Catalina) in Tacoronte (tel: 57 16 68).

Restaurants

There are several highly rated restaurants in La Laguna. For *tapas,* particularly cured meats, a limited range of meals and a choice of local wines, try the **Tasca La Carpintería** wine bar on Nuñez de la Peña 14, between Calle San Agustín and Calle Obispo Rey Redondo (tel: 26 30 56). The **Tasca-Restaurante La Gotera** (tel: 63 09 60), on the corner of Calle

San Agustín and Calle Viana, is also recommended. Just out of town the **Hoya del Camello**, Carretera General del Norte 128 (tel: 26 20 54), serves good Spanish and international dishes at reasonable prices.

San Andrés is famous for its fish and seafood restaurants, all of which huddle together on the seafront and in terms of quality there is little to choose between them. The best bet by the beach is the **Cofradía del Pescadores**, a pleasant small restaurant which shares the same building as the fishermen's bar-restaurant. The food at the popular *kioscos* on the beach is not recommended.

Shopping

La Laguna's main old-town shopping street is the Calle Obispo Rey Redondo, though most goods are for everyday local consumption. For a taste of a real country market call at the large **Mercado del Agricultor** on the Tacoronte–Tejina road, where local food and wine, including home-baked goodies, are on sale (*open*: Saturday 11.00–17.00hrs; Sunday 09.00–14.00hrs).

Special Events

After La Orotava (see page 46), La Laguna is the most important site on Tenerife for the **Corpus Christi** celebrations when its streets are decked in flowers and decorated with patterns made from coloured sands. Other colourful events include the **Fiesta y Romería de San Benito Abad** in La Laguna (first Sunday in July) and the **Romería de Tegueste** (northwest of La Laguna).

THE OROTAVA VALLEY

La Valle de la Orotava (the Orotava Valley), is not actually a valley at all but a great sloping plateau covering some 6–7 square miles (10–11sq km), rising above Puerto de la Cruz to just above La Orotava. On a clear day, with Mount Teide looming imperiously above all, this is one of the great sights of Tenerife. There are many good viewpoints onto La Valle but one of the finest is west of La Orotava at the **Mirador El Lance** just before Icod El Alto (on the TF221 road). From this lofty position the many buildings which have disfigured the valley (and which mar the traditional views from La Orotava) are reduced to insignificance on a mighty rolling green carpet. For many centuries La Orotava was the most important town of the northern region and up until the early 19th century the port, now known as Puerto de la Cruz, belonged to La Orotava and was called Puerto de la Orotava. Today La Orotava is still a wealthy town, but while the fortunes of Puerto de la Cruz have boomed with tourism, La Orotava has remained a backwater.

An unusually shaped Orotava blockhouse hides a gofio *mill*

office in La Orotava but the old town centre is compact and from the Plaza de la Constitución most points of interest are within a five- to ten-minute walk west (the Palacio Municipal may be able to supply you with a map).

What to See in La Orotava

♦♦♦
LA OROTAVA ✓

La Orotava is a beautifully preserved old colonial town of steep cobbled streets with architecture running the full gamut of styles from the last four centuries. It is a delightful place to discover on foot.
There is no tourist information

♦♦
CALLE SAN FRANCISCO

Walk up the steep hill past the Casas de los Balcones (see pages 42–3) and on the right is the **Hospital de la Santísima Trinidad** (Hospital of the Holy Trinity). Formerly an 18th-century convent, this is now a hospital which cares for the

Craftsmanship of the highest order at the Casas de los Balcones

mentally handicapped, though its courtyard is open to the public (Monday to Saturday 16.00–17.30hrs, Sunday 10.30hrs–noon). Notice the revolving drum set into the main door of the hospital. This type of door, not uncommon to old convents, was used to anonymously donate gifts and leave foundlings. There is a fine **view** from the terrace of the hospital over the Orotava Valley. Directly opposite the hospital is an attractive landscaped area with some old houses and just visible, behind a wall, is a curiously shaped pink building, topped with an orb. This is a flour mill, powered by water running down the steep incline, and one of many for which this district was once famous. Walk just a little way further up the hill, into Calle Dr González García, and at No 3 is an 18th-

century **flour mill** which produces and sells *gofio* (see **Food and Drink**, page 100). You are welcome to step inside its shop area and see part of the dusty workings and some old photographs of La Orotava.

◆◆◆
CASAS DE LOS BALCONES (HOUSES OF THE BALCONIES)
Calle San Francisco (tel: 38 28 55)
This beautiful colonial Canarian building, is named after the superbly crafted balconies which look onto the courtyard within, although the balconies on the front of the houses, dotted with red geraniums, are also very photogenic. The two houses, joined together, date from the 1630s and as you can see from the interesting upper-floor museum (entrance charge) were once home to a wealthy family. The ground floor is now a craft and souvenir shop, very popular for its traditionally dressed embroiderers and a wide range

of goods which attract coach parties from all over the island. At times the house can become uncomfortably overcrowded and is little more than a tourist trap. Yet the quality of its wares is generally high and craftsmen demonstrate the arts of cigar rolling by hand and basketry making. The interior courtyard is full of exotic greenery, an ancient wine press, and old pictures and pottery, conjuring up the atmosphere of colonial days most effectively.

Opposite is the **Casa del Turista** (also known as the Casa de la Alfombra), a house of similar style and age, built in 1590. It was formerly part of the Convento Molina (the Mill Convent) and there is a large cemetery immediately to the rear. This too is now a craft and gift shop, under the same management as the Casas de los Balcones, so its goods are very similar. There are two very good reasons for looking in even if you are not buying. Here you can see demonstrations of the sand-painting for which the town is famous at Corpus Christi time (see page 46), and from the rear terrace of the house there is an excellent view over the Valle de La Orotava.
Open: (both shops) Monday to Friday 09.00–13.30hrs and 16.00–19.30hrs; Saturday 09.00–13.30hrs.

◆◆
CENTRO CULTURAL CANARIO
Calle Carrera 17, off Calle San Francisco (tel: 32 27 25)
La Orotava's latest tourist venture is a promising small complex of museum, restaurant

(see page 45), *tasca* (snack bar) and craft shops, set in a house which dates from 1610. The museum, El Pueblo Guanche, is a lively history of the Guanche people complete with a mummy (text available in English).
Open: daily, 10.00–19.30hrs. (Restaurant and *tasca* open later Monday to Saturday.)

◆
IGLESIA DE NUESTRA SEÑORA DE LA CONCEPCIÓN (CHURCH OF OUR LADY OF THE IMMACULATE CONCEPTION)
Plaza Casañas
This extravagant, handsome baroque structure is a major landmark with twin onion-topped towers and a large yellow dome, built between 1768 and 1788. Its screen, altar (with an impressive tabernacle), *retablos* and carved choir stalls are generally regarded as masterpieces, though to the uninitiated eye, its dark interior with a peeling ceiling in need of repair, may be something of a disappointment.

◆◆◆
MUSEO DE ARTESANÍA IBEROAMERICANA (THE SPANISH AMERICAN HANDICRAFT MUSEUM)
Calle Tomás Zerolo 34, below Plaza de la Constitución (tel: 35 29 06)
The 17th-century Convento de Santo Domingo has been splendidly restored to house this wide-ranging collection of some fascinating and very colourful items from Latin America. Set in rooms around its cloisters are excellent

collections of ceramics, textiles, woodwork, musical instruments and basketwork. The highlight is the top floor which is devoted to popular art with some intriguing ritualistic objects (including several grotesque masks) associated with ceremonies and celebrations (for example, Mexico's Day of the Dead). Also on this floor are prize-winning pieces of modern Canarian handicraft and furniture design. Opposite the museum is the **Casa Torrehermosa**, another beautiful historic house, now home to *Art Tenerife*, an organisation showcasing high-quality island crafts.

Open: Museo de Artesanía: Monday to Saturday 09.30–18.00hrs; Casa Torrehermosa: Monday to Friday 09.30–18.00hrs; Saturday 09.30–14.00hrs.

◆◆
MUSEO DE CERÁMICA (POTTERY MUSEUM)

Carretera de la Luz-Las Candias, 1 mile (2km) west of La Orotava (tel: 33 33 96)

A collection of around 1,000 pieces of traditional Canarian and Spanish pottery is on display in this fine old house (Casa Tafuriaste) which dates from *c.*1600. Pottery-making demonstrations are also held.

Open: Monday to Saturday 10.00–18.00hrs.

◆◆
PALACIO MUNICIPAL (TOWN HALL)

Calle Carrera del Escultor Estevéz

This elegant building was designed in neo-classical style

between 1871 and 1891. It is the focus for the **Corpus Christi celebrations** with great carpets of flowers and coloured sands adorning the large square in front of it (see page 46). Enquire within for tourist information and a map of the town.

Immediately behind here is the **Hijuela del Botánico**. Its unusual name, 'Little Daughter of the Botanic Garden', explains its relationship with its famous parent near by in Puerto de la Cruz (see page 49). It is a small, densely planted area with over 3,000 different tropical and subtropical species including at least one very fine dragon tree. Disappointingly its gates are locked (though much of it can be seen from outside and visits can be made by special arrangement).

PLAZA DE LA CONSTITUCIÓN

This raised balcony-like square is the centre of the old town and the best place to start exploring. From here there is a marvellous roofscape of La Orotava, the foreground little changed for centuries though the further the view progresses to Puerto de la Cruz the more modern it becomes.

In a corner of the square is the **Iglesia San Agustín** (Church of St Augustine) with a handsome dark-stone bell tower and some fine *retablos*. The arch beneath the bell tower leads to what was once the monastery, and is now home to the **Conservatoria de Música** (Music School).

Set up on the hill at the back of the Plaza is the splendid pink-painted **Liceo de Taoro**. Its long

A strelitzia *(bird-of-paradise flower) in the Hijuela del Botánico*

entrance drive is reminiscent of a grand country house, or a gambling casino, adorned with beautiful gardens. The building dates from the 19th century and once functioned as a school. It is now a gentlemen's club but is frequently open to the public for art exhibitions and there is an elegant café-bar with balcony tables where you can sample a little of the high life. The entrance hall is very grand and whether or not you enjoy the temporary exhibition look out for the permanent picture collection (upstairs) of the *Romera Mayor* (La Orotava *romería* festival queens) which dates back to 1956.
Open: Liceo de Taoro: according to exhibition times.

Restaurants
La Orotava is not noted for its culinary delights but the newly opened restaurant at the **Centro Cultural Canario** (see page 43) may well be worth trying. Housed in the former stable of an early 17th-century house it is at once the city's oldest and newest eating place, serving authentic Canarian food. The comfortable **Bar Parada** in the corner of the Plaza de la Constitución serves *tapas* and full meals.

Children
Don't be tempted by the Oasis del Valle Botanic Zoo Park where large animals are kept in a thoroughly depressing collection of small concrete caged enclosures. The animals may be moved to more suitable premises in the near future leaving restaurants, gardens, donkey and camel rides.

Shopping
La Orotova is the official craft centre of the island and within the **Casas de los Balcones**, the **Casa del Turista** and the **Casa Torrehermosa** alone, just about every sort of Canarian craft item

is available. Casa Torrehermosa is the most expensive and its range is not extensive, but you may well pick up some handmade item that you won't see in the more mass-market shops. The **Museo de Artesanía Iberoamericana** also has a shop which has interesting items imported from Mexico and South America.

Special Events

La Orotava is famous for its **Corpus Christi** celebrations when specialist artists using coloured sands and flower petals turn the pavements into huge and colourful artworks. These are mostly floral or geometric but the occasional Old Master may also crop up. The most spectacular of all is laid out in front of the Palacio Municipal. These are only fleeting images, trampled underfoot by the devout during the religious processions, so if you are not visiting at this time of year look on postcards and visit the Casa del Turista to see how it is done.

Following hard on the heels of Corpus Christi is the *romería* season. The colourful **Romería of San Isidro** (see **Special Events**, page 108) is held in La Orotava in June. San Isidro is the patron saint of the island.

Work beginning on the Corpus Christi 'sand carpets' in La Orotava

PUERTO DE LA CRUZ

Puerto de la Cruz, or Puerto as everyone knows it, is the longest established and arguably the best all-round holiday resort on Tenerife. It has a magnificent backdrop, with Mount Teide towering above and the lush Orotava Valley sweeping down to the town.

Most importantly, unlike most Canarian resorts, this is a place with its own identity, where locals still live, work, eat, drink and relax. Puerto remains at heart a Spanish colonial town and despite the presence of some of the uglier aspects of Canarian mass tourism, it is still an enjoyable place in which to wander. Pick up a copy of *Puerto de la Cruz – Walking Through its Streets and Squares* from the tourist office.

The British put Puerto on the map as a holiday destination around a century ago, but today's town is very much abreast of the times with some top quality visitor attractions on its outskirts.

What to See in Puerto de la Cruz

◆◆◆

BANANERA EL GUANCHE

La Orotava/Autopista del Norte road; reached by a free bus or taxi service from Playa Martiánez (tel: 33 18 53)

This charming oasis is perfect for getting away from the hustle and noise of Puerto. A *bananera* is a banana plantation and a short video explains how the banana is cultivated before you start your self-guided tour.

The British were the first to introduce bananas to Tenerife

Bananas are only half the attraction here, for this is also a beautifully laid out botanic garden of exotic fruit trees and other plants. Mangos, kiwi fruit, passion fruit, pineapples, *tomateroes, chirimoyas* (custard apples), pomelos, papayas, avocados and *toronjas* (a giant grapefruit) all grow here. There's also the *zapote* (the chewing gum tree), sugar cane, macadamia trees, cocoa plants, over 400 cacti and many more indigenous and exotic species. (See also **Shopping**, page 56). *Open*: daily, 09.00–18.00hrs.

◆◆

CALLE/PASEO DE SAN TELMO

This charming popular promenade features the tiny, snow-white **Ermita de San**

Telmo (Hermitage of St Elmo)
which dates from 1780
(currently closed for
restoration). The sentry boxes
and teak fences here are relics
of the old Battery of St Elmo.
The town centre end of the
promenade is known as the
Punta del Viento (Windy Point),
and is marked by a modern
sculpture of a windswept girl.
Below, the waves break
spectacularly into the black-lava
rockpools.

◆
CASA IRIARTE
Calle San Juan
The famous Tenerife writer,
Tomás Iriarte (1750–91), after
whom this 18th-century house is
named, would be turning in his
grave if he knew the state of it
today. Once regarded as one of
the finest pieces of Canarian
architecture in Puerto, it has
been reduced to a tatty
shambles by its present owners
who run a cheap tourist shop on
the ground floor and, upstairs, a
badly lit naval museum. The
house still boasts a picturesque
balcony projecting onto the
street and a lovely interior patio,
and is still worth a visit.
On the pretty square diagonally
opposite is the Colegio San
Agustín. This occupies the 18th-
century **Palacio Ventoso**, with
its landmark tower (currently
under restoration).
Open: Casa Iriarte: Monday to
Saturday 09.30–18.00hrs.

◆◆
CASINO TAORO
Parque Taoro
The building that now houses
the Casino Taoro began life in
1892 as the Grand Hotel Taoro,
at the time the largest hotel in all
of Spanish territory and the
most prestigious hotel in all the
islands. A disastrous fire in
1929 effectively put an end to
its career and in 1975 it became
the Casino Taoro. Gamblers
and gourmets beat a path here
by night (see **Culture,
Entertainment and Nightlife**,
pages 54–5, and **Restaurants**,
page 56) but what makes the
trip worthwhile by day is the
Risco Bello Jardín Acuático
(Aquatic Gardens). There are
three levels to these water
gardens with a lovely lake on
the first level, but not a lot else.
The lawned café garden
(entrance free) is absolutely

Mount Teide looming above the splendid Lido Martiánez

delightful and provides a perfect oasis from the noise and bustle down below.
Open: Risco Bello Jardín Acuático: daily, 09.30–18.30hrs; Casino Taoro: opening hours given on page 55.

◆◆ IGLESIA DE SAN FRANCISCO (CHURCH OF ST FRANCIS)
Calle de Quintana
This beautiful church was originally built between 1599 and 1608, making it the oldest building in the centre of Puerto. It features some glowing *retablos*.

◆◆ JARDÍN BOTÁNICO (BOTANIC GARDEN)
Calle Retama, off Carretera del Botánico (tel: 38 52 72)
This is the oldest of Puerto's many attractions, founded in 1788 by order of King Carlos III as the *Jardín de Aclimatación de La Orotava* (Acclimatisation Garden of Orotava), a halfway-house for plants travelling from the tropics to Spain. The experiment was a failure as the second part of the journey, to Europe, proved too cold for many species. The garden became an important place of botanic study and is now a popular visitor attraction.
It's a relatively small and very shady place with over 200 species of plants and trees (but very few flowers), crowding into just 6 acres (2.5ha). The favourite specimen is the giant 200-year old South American fig tree in the centre, a Gothic spider's web of intertwined roots and branches.
Open: daily, 09.00–18.00hrs.

◆◆◆ LIDO/LAGO DE MARTIÁNEZ (LIDO/POOL OF MARTIÁNEZ)
Playa Martiánez (tel: 38 38 52)
Although Puerto has long been a popular seaside holiday resort, for many years the lack of a decent beach meant there was no pleasant public area for sunbathing and swimming. This problem was addressed over 25 years ago by César Manrique (see box, page 50), who was commissioned to design this lido. The result is a highly acclaimed, beautifully laid out complex of pools and

César Manrique

The greatest modern Canarian artist and designer, César Manrique (1919–92) is most famous for his work on Lanzarote. The hallmark of all his visitor attractions and designs is that they are in harmony with the natural landscape. Formerly in great demand throughout the islands (and on mainland Spain) his major completed projects on Tenerife include the Lido de Martiánez and Playa Jardín (both in Puerto). At the time of his death he was also working on the Parque Marítimo in Santa Cruz and the Mirador del Palmarejo on La Gomera.

fountains, palm-shaded sunbathing terraces and a black and white lava rockery which covers over 7 acres (3ha). The central fountain, which erupts regularly, is a favourite feature. *Open*: daily, 09.00–18.00hrs.

◆◆◆
LORO PARQUE (PARROT PARK) ✓

Calle San Felipe (tel: 37 38 41); free buses from Playa Martiánez and Playa de las Américas
The popular Loro Parque is the most publicised and the most

The Thai Village – inspired by a visit by the Prince of Siam in 1914

expensive attraction on the island. Since its foundation in 1972 it has attracted over 11 million visitors and provides a memorable and enjoyable day out for the whole family. As its name suggests, it began life solely as a parrot park and today houses the largest collection in the world, numbering some 300 species with breeding programmes to conserve endangered varieties. Since 1992 it has become a major wildlife and zoo park, operated with a very high level of professionalism.

The magnificent tropical gardens in which the park stands cover an area of around 31 acres (12.5ha) with over 2,000 palm trees. Today the most popular park residents are the sea lions and the dolphins which give a marvellous show. Equally impressive is the splendid aquarium and it is impossible not to feel a frisson of

A Blue and gold macaw originating from South America

terror as you walk through one of the world's largest underwater tunnels and 6-foot (2m) sharks glide silently within inches of your face.

Other highlights include the gorilla colony, the nocturnal bat cave, Tiger Island and, of course, the parrot shows. There is also Lorovision, a simulator thrill-ride, which with the aid of a 180-degree special-effects cinema, starts with a stomach-churning roller-coaster ride and then takes you on various other frightening aerial experiences. The park's latest venture is Natura Vision, a spell-binding special-effects film which flies the viewer through the Spanish national parks, over Mount Teide, on to Florida's Key West and finally to Venezuela and the Orinoco river rainforest. *Open*: daily, 08.30–17.00hrs.

◆
MUSEO ARQUEOLÓGICO (ARCHAEOLOGICAL MUSEUM)

Calle de Lomo 9 (tel: 37 14 65)
Housed in a fine 19th-century mansion this small museum stages temporary exhibitions, usually relating to the Guanche culture. Even if archaeology isn't your thing it's well worth a walk around this part of town, particularly **Calle San Felipe**, which is full of old single-storey fishermen's houses and lots of good local restaurants.
Open: Tuesday to Saturday 10.00–13.00hrs and 17.00–21.00hrs; Sunday 10.00–13.00hrs.

◆◆
PLAYA JARDÍN

This attractive new black-sand beach was opened in 1992 and, like the Lido Martiánez, it was landscaped under the direction of César Manrique (see box, page 50) with lovely gardens and one of his signature sculptures. The crashing Atlantic waves have been tamed by a man-made reef comprising some 4,000 20-ton concrete blocks (which are submerged). Bathers should always take care due to the often rough sea, which also means watersports are out of the question here. Adjacent is the 17th-century **Castillo de San Felipe**. The interior of this handsome, small, four-square fortress has been beautifully restored to function as a cultural centre where temporary art exhibitions and concerts (see **Culture, Entertainment and Nightlife**, page 55) are held.

Open: times vary according to temporary exhibitions. Contact the tourist office (tel: 38 60 00) for details. There are concerts most Saturdays at 20.30hrs.

◆◆
PLAZA DEL CHARCO

Sooner or later everyone comes to this handsome raised square. It is the heart of the town, shaded by huge Indian laurel trees brought over from Cuba in 1852, and is always lively with buskers, street sellers or locals doing the *paseo*. Holiday-makers look on from the Café Dinámico. The **Rincón del Puerto**, is a beautiful, typical Canarian balconied courtyard, built in 1739, now full of eating and drinking places.

◆◆◆
PLAZA IGLESIA

This is Puerto's loveliest plaza with an elegant swan fountain in the centre, dating from 1900. The **Iglesia de la Peña de Francia** (Church of the Rock of France) is a beautiful 16th-century building (its tower was added in 1898) with excellent baroque altarpieces and side-chapels. Note the pulpit – wooden, but cleverly painted to resemble marble.
The **Hotel Marquesa** (built 1712) and the **Hotel Monopol** (built 1742) both possess typical balconied patios. Take a look inside. The tourist information office is also on the square.

◆◆◆
PUERTO PESQUERO (FISHING PORT)

Just below the Plaza del Charco is a small but colourful working

fishing port. The beautiful-
black-and-white stone house is
the **Casa de la Real Aduana**
(Royal Custom House), one of
the oldest buildings in town,
dating from 1620, and until 1833
functioning as the Customs
House (closed to the public).
Behind here are the
fortifications of the **Battery of
Santa Bárbara**, built in the mid-
18th century.
On the opposite side of the
street is the beautifully restored
Casa de Miranda, dating from
around 1730. This was the house
of the Venezuelan liberator,
Francisco Miranda (whose
statue stands in the square at the
far end of the Calle San Telmo)
and it now houses a very
pleasant bar and restaurant.
A little further on is a new
square with old cannons, the
Plaza de Europe, from where
there are good sea views. To

*The Casa de la Real Aduana (left)
still guards the harbour*

the right are the **Casas
Consistoriales** (town hall
offices), built 1973. On weekday
mornings traditionally dressed
ladies sell flowers here, most
notably strelitzias, at a fraction of
the price offered by tourist
establishments (though not
boxed).

Accommodation
There is a very wide choice of
3- and 4-star hotels in Puerto.
The most beautiful and most
traditional are the **Marquesa**
(tel: 38 31 51) and the **Monopol**
(tel: 38 46 11), both of which are
3-star rated and occupy 18th-
century Canarian buildings on
Plaza Iglesia. Be warned though,
this can be a noisy part of town
with no car parking and some
rooms are fairly basic. Perhaps

the best choice for peace and quiet within walking distance of the centre is the 4-star **Hotel Tigaiga** (tel: 38 35 00) in the Parque Taoro Casino grounds. If you would like to go native, courtesy of the recent rural tourism initiative, there are traditional houses for rent at Santa Ursula and La Matanza, just outside Puerto; contact ATREA for details (tel: 57 00 15).

Children
Loro Parque is a must for all ages while water babies will love the **Lido Martiánez**. The **Bananera El Guanche** may be of interest, particularly to older children.

Culture, Entertainment and Nightlife
Puerto may lack the number of discotheques of the south but for a broad range of nocturnal entertainment it is the liveliest place on the island. Look in the *Tenerife Holiday Gazette* for details and keep an eye open

for fly posters. The Parque San Francisco, opposite the Iglesia de San Francisco, is a popular all-purpose venue and there are several bars which feature live Spanish or Canarian guitar groups (generally advertised by posters in the bar windows).

Casino
The **Casino Taoro** (tel: 38 05 50) is the oldest and grandest gambling house on the islands. French and American roulette, blackjack (pontoon) and craps are the most common games. The rules are explained before each session, though that probably won't stop you losing your money. Here are two common-sense rules to cut your losses: decide on your limit in advance and stick to it rigidly; leave your credit cards at the hotel! Once you're out of notes, slot machines will gobble up your loose change.

Solidified lava off the weather-beaten shoreline of Puerto de la Cruz

You must be at least 18 years old, carry your passport and dress smartly (though not necessarily in jacket and tie) to be admitted.
Open: Monday to Friday 20.00–03.00hrs; Saturday and Sunday 20.00–04.00hrs.

Concerts

The atmospheric interior of the **Castillo San Felipe** (see **Playa Jardín**, page 52) is a charming place to listen to piano recitals, string quartets and other small-scale concerts. Banners on the outside of the castle advertise forthcoming events.

Discotheques

The **El Coto Up & Down**, at the Oro Negro Hotel on Avenida de Colón, and the **Victoria**, also on Avenida de Colón, are two of the best in town.

Folklore

The best place to catch a folklore performance is in the gardens of the **Hotel Tigaiga**,

Parque Taoro (behind the Casino) at 11.00hrs each Sunday morning (tel: 38 35 00).

Nightclubs and Shows

The Lido Martiánez plays host nightly to the **Isla del Lago Andromeda Show Internacional**, starring flamenco dancers and a bevy of bare-breasted feather-clad dancing beauties (tel: 38 38 52). There is more exotic dancing by the African National Ballet at **La Cueva**, which is a real cave, with fine sea views, near Los Realejos (tel: 34 08 05). A different set of dancers also perform a Hawaiian show. The **Tenerife Palace** at Las Cabezas (tel: 37 48 96) also features 'Hawaiian' entertainment plus Ballet Español and flamenco dancing.

Restaurants

Puerto is an excellent place to eat out with an enormous choice of restaurants catering to all tastes and budgets, including a good number of local establishments. The best place to head for the latter is the old fishermen's quarter, centring on Calle de San Felipe and Calle de Lomo. The most famous place here is **Mi Vaca y Yo** at Calle Cruz Verde 3a (dinner only, tel: 38 52 47). This is a charming rustic Canarian for excellent local (and international) cuisine, particularly seafood **Restaurante Regu¹** atmospheric and recommended tel: 38 45 06). In the centre del Charc

Good-value leather can be found almost everywhere on the island

courtyard offers a number of options including **Mario** (tel: 38 55 35), which is good for fish. Just out of the centre at Carretera del Botánico 5, (Urbanización La Paz) **Magnolia** (tel: 38 56 14) serves acclaimed Catalan and international dishes. Close by on Camino El Durazno is **Casa Lala** (tel: 38 17 94), serving excellent Canarian food. At Santa Ursula, just outside town, serving top quality international cuisine to ex-pats and locals, are **El Lagar** (tel: 30 75), and **Los Corales** (tel: 30) the latter specialising in h are on Carretera e la Villa.
with deep wallets and th Lady Luck on uld note that the nt (tel: 37 26 60) for classic , and enjoys o.
mple

tastes, one of the best and most attractive *tapas* bars in town is friendly **Cafetería Arcon**, Calle Blanco 8.

Shopping
Leather lovers should beat a path to the factory-outlet **Ladi Centre** at nearby Santa Ursula. The **Bananera El Guanche** is a good place to buy *strelitzias* and tropical fruits, specially boxed for the aircraft cargo hold.

Special Events
Aside from Santa Cruz, Puerto is the best place to be on Tenerife for *Carnaval* (see pages 28, 29 and 109–10). The Plaza del Charco becomes a huge *salsa* dance area and the Burial of the Sardine is a splendidly bizarre affair, culminating at the Puerto Pesquero.
On 15 July the **Fiestas del Gran Poder de Dios** are the town's second biggest annual event, celebrated with the usual energy, including processions and fireworks.

MOUNT TEIDE AND THE CUMBRE DORSAL

Mount Teide is the highlight of Tenerife in every sense, featuring some of the world's most dramatic volcanic landscapes. It is not only the high spot of this island and of this archipelago, but at 12,198 feet (3,718m) it's the highest point in all Spanish territory. Not surprisingly it can be seen (weather permitting) from almost anywhere on the island. Its classic triangular snow-covered peak is a ubiquitous backdrop for postcards, and has become the unofficial island trademark.

There are four ways of approaching the mighty mountain: from La Orotava; from the east, along the Cumbre Dorsal; from the west; and from the south. Each route brings stunning new vistas with every twist and turn of the road. The landscape around the mountain also changes dramatically with the seasons, from gentle flower carpets in summer to a harsh icy wilderness in winter.

◆◆◆
CUMBRE DORSAL ✓

The least travelled, but arguably the most spectacular of the four Mount Teide routes is along the Cumbre Dorsal, the great volcanic ridge which forms the backbone of the island. There is only one road, known as the Carretera Dorsal, which runs from La Laguna to El Portillo. The first settlement south of La Laguna along this way is

Going up – the easy way, but beware winter stoppages

Weather in the Park

Conditions in the Parque Nacional del Teide vary dramatically between winter and summer. In winter there are snowfalls, gale-force winds blow and the roads are sometimes closed. In summer this arid landscape is aglow with plants and flowers and daytime temperatures can soar above 104°F (40°C), though on the summit of Teide it is still chilly.

Don't worry too much if your journey from the coast is mostly in the clouds. Generally just before you near the cable car station these will part to reveal bright blue skies and the omnipresent mountain.

La Esperanza. The village itself
is of no great tourist interest but
it does mark the start of the
Bosque de la Esperanza, a
dense and beautiful forest of
Canary pines. This is fertile
walking territory with several
waymarked trails, famous as the
place where in 1936 General
Franco came to meet his fellow
Civil War conspirators (see
page 14). An obelisk marks the
fateful tryst at the spot known as
Las Raíces (signposted, just off
the main road) where there is
also a café.

Shortly after this are the first two
viewpoints. There is no
official *mirador* at **Montaña
Grande**, 3,675 feet (1,120m),
but there is space to pull off the
road for a wide panorama down
to Santa Cruz. Next comes the
Mirador Pico de las Flores, at
4,300 feet (1,310m), enjoying
views to La Laguna and the
Anaga mountains. After another
4½ miles (7km) the **Mirador de
Ortuño**, at 5,920 feet (1,820m),
offers the first opportunity to see
Mount Teide. The best views of
all are from the **Mirador de
Los Cumbres**, where there are
actually two *miradores*; the one
to the south reveals the Bosque
de la Esperanza in all its glory;
the magnificent view to the north
takes in Teide.

It's worth pausing for a view of
the **Caldera de Pedro Gil**,
shortly before the strange white
shapes of the **Insitituto de
Astrofísica de Canarias/
Observatorio de Izaña**
(astrophysics institute and
observatory) at Izaña start to
loom on the horizon. There is no
public entry to this research
station but it's well worth making

a short detour off the main road
for a closer look at these
gleaming space-age structures.

◆◆
PAISAJE LUNAR (LUNAR LANDSCAPE)

Almost the whole of the Parque
Nacional del Teide resembles a
lunar landscape but the so-
called Paisaje Lunar is the
strangest of all the rock
formations. It comprises a series
of light brown tufa columns
which are unique to the Canary
Islands. Their swirling surreal
conical shapes are reminiscent
of the work of the famous
Spanish architect Gaudí. You
can only get to the Paisaje Lunar
on foot from the Campamento
del Madre (4½ miles/7km there
and back). To reach the
Campamento take the track
2½ miles/4km north of Vilaflor.

MOUNT TEIDE AND THE CUMBRE DORSAL

Mount Teide, seemingly floating above the clouds – as seen from the neighbouring island of Gran Canaria

◆◆◆
PARQUE NACIONAL DEL TEIDE (MOUNT TEIDE NATIONAL PARK) ✓

Some 3 million years ago a giant volcano close to where Teide is now (but much bigger than Teide) exploded and probably collapsed in on itself. The volcano walls, or what is left of them, formed a *caldera* (crater) in which Teide, and other volcanoes, now stand. The *caldera* has a diameter of 10 miles (16km), measures some 28 miles (45km) in circumference and some parts of the wall still stand up to 1,640 feet (500m) high. From ground level it is impossible to fully

appreciate the scale of events but as you gaze upon the torn and twisted earth it is clear that whatever caused this possessed an awesome degree of power. Not surprisingly this apocalyptic, lunar-like appearance has been eagerly seized upon by film makers who have used it for *The Ten Commandments*, *Planet of the Apes* and for *One Million Years BC*.

In 1954 the Caldera, which covers some 33,000 acres (13,500ha), and the summit (Pico del Teide), was declared a national park and protected from any development. Most visitors approach Teide from north or south, thus missing the fascinating landscapes of the road west to Chio. Points of interest on this route include **Las Lavas Negras** (the black lava fields) and a view of **Las Narices del Teide** (the nostrils of Teide)

MOUNT TEIDE AND THE CUMBRE DORSAL

which blew in 1898, the volcano's most recent eruption. Further along this road are the distinctive cones of several extinct volcanoes and a good view of the island of La Gomera.

Los Roques de García (The Rocks of García)

Los Roques is the most spectacular grouping of pyroclastic debris within the Park and is probably a part of the walls of the old volcano. Set just a few yards from the main road, it is on every coach tour itinerary and the rocks are often swarming with day trippers. It would be hard to detract from such a magnificent sight as this though, with views to Teide one side and to the other the great flat expanse of the plain of **Llano de Ucanca**. This is the most famous of the Park's many *cañadas* – yellow-coloured sedimentary plains where fine debris has accumulated. From the far side of the Llano de Ucanca is the classic picture-postcard view of Mount Teide and Los Roques. Situated across the road from Los Roques is the Parador Nacional de las Cañadas (see **Accommodation** and **Restaurants**, page 62). Close to Los Roques, heading south, is the rock formation known as **Los Azulejos** where the rocks glint blue-green with iron hydrate deposits.

Pico del Teide

It's a strenuous but exhilarating experience to walk to the top of Mount Teide and takes around three hours. You should be fit and wear warm clothing and stout footwear. It is vital to call at

El Portillo (see pages 61–2) for advice on accessibility – routes are open and closed, seemingly at random. You must never undertake this ascent in poor weather and inexperienced walkers should not attempt it at all in winter. It is also important to know whether **el teleférico** (the cable car) is running on the day of your climb. All too often it is out of action in winter for maintenance, or when it is too icy or too windy. It is also far better to walk up and take the cable car down (rather than vice versa). If the car is not running, you face a strenuous descent on already tired legs. Never assume that the car is in service simply because you see it running; it may well just be carrying maintenance staff. The ascent begins at the car park below **Montaña Blanca**, which is signposted off the main park road. It takes around 60 to 75 minutes to reach the top of the White Mountain and by the time you get to this first summit you should have a good idea whether you can cope with the rest of the climb. If not, then your journey hasn't been wasted as Montaña Blanca is a very worthwhile climb in its own right. From here your route takes you past the huge black round volcanic boulders, known as **Los Huevos del Teide** (literally, the 'Eggs of Teide'), the mountain refuge of **Refugio de Altavista**, the **Cueva del Hielo** (ice cave), and up past smouldering sulphurous blowholes where you can warm your hands on the dormant volcano's heat. Disappointingly the actual summit is closed for long-term repairs leaving you 531 feet (162m) short of the top (at the platform to which the cable car ascends). The views are magnificent and on a clear day you can see Gran Canaria, El Hierro and La Palma, as well as La Gomera.

Of course the vast majority of Teide's visitors ascend and descend the mountain the easy way, by cable car, moving from the base camp at 7,730 feet (2,356m) to 11,663 feet (3,555m) in just eight minutes. However, the car takes only a few passengers at a time and long queues often form.

For cable car information telephone 38 37 11/28 78 37.

It operates daily from 09.00–16.00hrs, weather permitting.

◆
EL PORTILLO VISITORS' INFORMATION CENTRE
19 miles (32km) south of Puerto de la Cruz

For anyone seeking an insight into Tenerife's greatest natural showcase, El Portillo (the gateway) will come as a disappointment. There is a film (with English commentary) which covers all the national parks in the Canaries, plus a

Los Roques, the eroded remains of volcanic rock, are an obligatory stop on everyone's Teide Grand Tour

MOUNT TEIDE AND THE CUMBRE DORSAL

series of panels and a couple of models relating to the geology and natural history of the Park. There is very little information in English and the staff are usually not very helpful.

The best reason for coming to El Portillo is to join one of the walking tours which depart from here, led by an experienced guide. The tours are free but you must reserve your place (tel: 29 01 29/29 01 83). Given the rather disorganised nature of this office, ask a Spanish-speaking person to make the call for you and to confirm whether or not the guide speaks English. If not it is probably still worth joining the tour as the scenery is the main attraction. If you intend walking on your own in the Park you should still call in here for maps and advice. Note that walking in the Park can be very dangerous in winter.
Open: Monday to Friday 09.00–13.30hrs and 14.30–16.00hrs.

Accommodation

There is only one hotel in the Park and that is the **Parador Nacional de las Cañadas** (tel:

The new improved Parador Nacional de las Cañadas is the perfect base for walking in the National Park

38 64 15). Located opposite Los Roques this has always been a perfect base for walking in the Park. In recent years its rather basic 2-star facilities became run down and a major refurbishment was undertaken in 1996. It is expected that when it is re-opened the mountain chalet character will be unaffected but it will be a lot more comfortable and will be upgraded to a 3-star rating.

Restaurants

There are few restaurants within this area. The **Restaurante Boca del Tauce** (tel: 85 05 29), just outside the Parque Nacional boundary on the Chio road, serves good quality local and international food in a friendly and prompt fashion. The **Parador** (see **Accommodation**, above) is also an excellent place for Spanish and Canarian dishes, but do book ahead (tel: 38 64 15).

THE NORTHWEST

The Teno Massif (Teno Hills) make the northwest corner of Tenerife one of its most picturesque areas and despite the coachloads who make this trip daily, the narrow precipitous road to Masca still makes for an adventure. Icod de los Vinos also attracts the crowds but even if you have seen a hundred pictures of its famous dragon tree the real thing will still astonish you. By contrast Garachico is quiet, and is the most charming, unspoilt small town on Tenerife.

BUENAVISTA DEL NORTE
6 miles (10km) west of Icod de los Vinos
The name means 'fine views of the north' but it's not worth trying to seek them out here – they are much better at the **Punta de Teno**, 7 miles (11km) west, and *en route* at the **Mirador de Don Pompeyo**. This neat and tidy small town is a good place for a coffee stop, particularly in the pretty square

next to the bandstand, sitting with the locals. Opposite, the church of Nuestra Señora de los Remedios (Our Lady of Remedies) has a fine *mudéjar* ceiling.
The Punta de Teno is the westernmost point of Tenerife with a lighthouse and a small rocky beach. From there are fine views extending south as far as Los Gigantes.

◆◆◆ GARACHICO✓

19 miles (31km) west of Puerto de la Cruz (via El Tanque)
Garachico was founded in 1496 by the Genoese banker Cristóbal de Ponte and for over 200 years it flourished as the island's major port, exporting mostly wine. It became extremely rich and was home to members of the aristocracy and wealthy merchants. But in 1706 its prosperity vanished overnight. Lava spilled out of the Volcán Negra volcano, down to,

The lava-choked former harbour of old Garachico

The Parque Puerto de Tierra, once the gateway to the port

the sea at Garachico, filling and thus destroying its superb natural harbour. Much of the town was also destroyed though some of its ancient homes do still survive. Rebuilding took place on the newly formed lava peninsula in the early 18th century and since then Garachico has changed little. The best place to see the path of the molten destruction is from high above the town at the **Mirador de Garachico** (on the C820 from Icod de los Vinos). This offers a marvellous, much-photographed aerial view of the town and its tiny offshore islet, **Roque de Garachico**. Notice the cross on top of the Rock, placed there to protect the town against another such disaster. It takes motorists 6 miles (9km) of winding hairpin road to make the descent of the hillside via El Tanque. (As you drive down notice the grassy cone of an old

volcano to your left.) The lava took the direct route as you will see when you get to the bottom and look back up.

The tourist office is in the El Limonero Artesanía (Handicrafts Centre) on the seafront opposite the castle, and they can provide you with an excellent leaflet mapping all the major points of interest.

The most notable survivor of the disaster is the beautifully preserved **Castillo de San Miguel** (Castle of St Michael) which dates from the 16th century. It now houses a small museum of fossils, mineral, rocks and shells (*open*: daily, 09.00–18.00hrs). The lava which swam then solidified around the base of the castle, has now been landscaped into an attractive swimming pool and garden area.

Close by is the port, which still functions, albeit on a relatively small scale. On the road above it (going to Buenavista del Norte) is a poignant modern

memorial dedicated to the Canary Island emigrants, many of whom sailed to the New World from Garachico. Before 1706 the port extended much further into the town and the 16th-century gateway arch to the old port was excavated and re-erected where it originally stood. Today it is surrounded by a charming square and a beautiful sunken garden, named the **Parque Puerto de Tierra**. The picturesque 17th-century wine press here is a reminder of how important the wine trade was to Garachico. From the garden is a picture-postcard view of the **Iglesia de Santa Ana** (Church of St Anna), part-buried by the lava and rebuilt in the 18th century. It boasts an outstanding *retablo* and its interior has just been refurbished.

Continue past here to the delightful main town square where there is a fine bandstand and to the right-hand side the **Casa Palacio de los Condes de la Gomera** (the Palace of the Counts of Gomera). This 17th-century house has seen better days and is currently being restored. The **Iglesia de San Francisco** (Church of St Francis) dates from the 16th century and is beautiful within and without. The adjacent former Franciscan convent now functions as the **Casa de Cultura**, set around two courtyards, one of which is beautifully planted with slender palms and rose trees. Old pictures of Garachico emphasise how little the town has changed and there are also rag-bag collections of natural history and ethnography items.

(*Open*: Monday to Friday 09.00–19.00hrs; Saturday 09.00–18.00hrs; Sunday 09.00–13.00hrs.) There is a statue in the square of the famous South American liberator, Simón Bolívar, whose mother came from Garachico. At the far end of town the dark and ancient interior of the 17th-century **Convento de Santo Domingo** is now home to the **Museo de Arte Contemporáneo** (Museum of Contemporary Art) containing some startling modern exhibits. (*Open*: daily, 09.00–13.00hrs and 15.00–18.00hrs.)

◆◆◆
LOS GIGANTES/PUERTO DE SANTIAGO
25 miles (42km) north of Playa de las Américas
A quiet, low-rise, tightly packed holiday development has

Los Gigantes ('the Giants') sea cliffs

sprung up here, huddling on the small bay opposite the dramatic sea-cliffs which are known as Los Gigantes (see below). It is a pleasant place with whitewashed buildings in local style and flower-filled gardens but it is crammed with English bars and any local atmosphere has disappeared.

Sightseeing interest (aside from the cliffs) centres on boat trips to spot dolphins and whales (see box, page 77). The most picturesque vessel is the *Katrin*, built in 1940 as a working fishing boat. You can also arrange walking tours of the Barranco de Masca from here, with the all-important pick-up boat waiting for you at the bottom of the gorge (see **Masca**, page 69).

Los Gigantes ('the Giants') are an awesome sight and drop almost sheer into the sea from a height of around 1,650–2,000 feet (500–600m). Wait until a boat passes in front of them and see how it is reduced to a mere insignificant speck.

Los Gigantes merge almost seamlessly into Puerto de Santiago which is known for its black-sand beach, **Playa de la Arena**, landscaped with gardens and fledgling palms, and kept spotlessly clean. Swimmers should take care as there is a dangerous undertow. For some ethnic interest follow the road inland to Arguayo to the **Centro Alfarero**. Here you will see ceramics made by hand without the use of a potter's wheel, in the manner of the Guanches (see also **El Cercado, La Gomera**, pages 85–6). *Open*: Monday to Saturday 10.00–13.00hrs and 16.00–19.00hrs.

Here Be Dragons!

Dragon trees (*Dracaena draco*) date back to the days of the dinosaurs and are only found in the Macronesian islands of the Canaries, the Azores and the Madeiran archipelago. With clusters of deadly looking sword-shaped leaves and a resin that turns red on exposure to the air it is perhaps not surprising that the Guanches attributed magical properties to dragon trees. They used its bark for war shields, its red 'dragon's blood' sap to heal wounds, to embalm their dead and to ward off evil spirits, and when the trees blossomed this was thought to herald a good harvest.

Even today magical properties are associated with 'dragon's blood', including the ability to cure leprosy. After the Spanish Conquest it found its way to Italy where it was used as a dye and a stain for marble.

Another peculiarity of these spiky giants is that they have no growth rings. It is not even possible to date the tree accurately by its branch count, as there is much argument about where one branch starts and another one ends – hence the debate about the age of Icod de los Vinos' great specimen (see page 67), which is popularly claimed to be anywhere between one and three thousand years old, but may in fact only date back to the 16th century.

If you would like a dragon tree of your own the shops by the tree sell seeds and despite jokes about having to wait a thousand years they do grow remarkably quickly.

◆◆◆
ICOD DE LOS VINOS ✓

13 miles (22km) west of Puerto de la Cruz

Icod de los Vinos is famous above all else for its **Drago Milenario**, which translates as '1,000-year-old dragon tree'. The real age of this monster is unknown (see box, page 66) but it is certainly the oldest dragon tree in existence and despite the concrete which shores up its base it is still very much alive. At over 52 feet (16m) tall and with a girth of 18 feet (6m) it is the largest too. By way of comparison look up the hill to see another very fine specimen.

The obvious view of the tree is from the **Plaza de la Iglesia**, which can be mayhem when coach parties arrive – and they do, frequently. There is a picture-postcard view from the other side which includes an exceedingly tall palm tree and a typical Canarian balcony. At the time of your visit the area around the tree may be fenced off as work is underway to build a park to give the tree the natural setting it deserves. The Plaza de la Iglesia boasts some exotic greenery of its own: notice the splendid *Pandanus utilis* trees from Madagascar. The beautiful 15th- to 16th-century **Iglesia de San Marco** (Church of St Mark) on the square is famous for its treasury which holds a magnificent silver cross from Mexico. It is over 6 feet (2m) tall and is a masterpiece of silver filigree work. The church also features an outstanding 17th-century *retablo* and beautiful coffered ceilings.

As its name suggests Icod de los Vinos is also renowned for its wine and you will have the chance to sample this, free of

The fiercest of them all – the great dragon tree of Icod de los Vinos next to the Iglesia de San Marco

THE NORTHWEST

charge, in either the Casa del
Drago (by the Plaza de la
Iglesia) or at one of the two
shops on the adjacent **Plaza
del Pilar**. This is a charming
shady square, remarkably
unaffected by all the bustle
going on a few feet away.
If a swim appeals after your
wine tasting and sightseeing,
Playa de San Marcos is a
pleasant black-sand beach
with restaurants and fishing
boats, just below the town.

MASCA ✓

*12 miles (20km) southwest of
Garachico*
The tip of the northwest is

*Masca – no longer hidden but still
a treasure*

covered by the **Teno Massif**
(Teno Hills) – one of the most
picturesque corners of the
island, rent by deep ravines and
cloaked in lush greenery. The
road leading south from
Buenavista del Norte is one of
the most spectacular on the
island – very narrow, very steep
and with some incredibly tight
hairpin bends. Only recently has
the road been built and now the
shangri-la village of Masca is on
most coach excursion
itineraries. Fortunately its
magical site, set on narrow
ridges which plunge down into a
verdant valley of dramatic rock

formations, is impossible to diminish. And, happily, aside from a handful of shops and idyllically positioned bars which have sprung up to take advantage of this new fortune, the outward appearance of the village hasn't changed much either. Nonetheless, at certain times it is overwhelmed by visitors, so to see it in its natural peaceful condition, come either early or late in the day.

The beautiful **Barranco de Masca**, the valley which leads from the village to the sea, is becoming something of a tourist attraction in its own right. It's a two-hour walk down but a four-hour walk back up so unless you are a very keen walker it makes sense to arrange for a boat to collect you at the bottom (see **Los Gigantes**, page 66). Accidents do happen in this *barranco* and only experienced walkers should attempt the walk on their own. Others should enlist the services of a guide. Disappointingly (for drivers) there are few *miradores* around Masca but spectacular views can be enjoyed at the high pass south of Masca, just before Santiago del Teide. To the east is a splendid **view** of Mount Teide. Back to the south is the strange sight of an old red volcano with slices cut away from it with almost geometrical precision. Too neat for nature, this is the work of man, harvesting the volcano for its rich ash for fertiliser and its rocks for building materials.

Accommodation

If you want to stay in style at Los Gigantes the 4-star **Gigantes-**

Los Stil, Flor de Pascua (tel: 10 10 20) is the resort's top hotel, with all the relevant facilities. The rest of the conurbation is mostly apartments.

There is very little tourist accommodation in the rest of this region though one of the island's most promising establishments has just opened at Garachico. The **Hotel San Roque** (tel: 13 34 35) on Calle Esteban de Ponte is a beautiful conversion of the 18th-century Casa de Ponte, a typical grand Canarian house with a fine courtyard. Modern comforts in each of its 18 rooms and suites include air-conditioning, satellite TV and the loan of videos and compact disc players, belying its 3-star rating.

Children

The **dragon tree** of Icod de los Vinos may impress them briefly but the best bet for children is the **Camello Center**, just above Garachico in the town of El Tanque. Camel caravans depart regularly, there are *burro* (donkey) safaris and you can take mint tea in an authentic Arab tent. (*Open*: daily 10.00–18.00hrs.) It's best to book ahead (tel: 83 11 91).

Restaurants
Garachico

The **Isla Baja** (tel: 83 00 08) on the seafront is a long established favourite, specialising in fish dishes, but it is expensive. For good down-to-earth Canarian cooking at low prices go to the charming **Bodegón Plaza** (tel: 83 09 77), a Canarian house with several rooms where typical island food

is served in a quiet friendly atmosphere (Calle Estaban de Ponte). **Casa Ramón** (tel: 83 00 77), also on Calle Esteban de Ponte, is similar in character.

Icod de Los Vinos
Carmen (tel: 81 06 31), just below the Plaza de la Iglesia, is probably the best restaurant in this part of town. It is a beautifully restored traditional house serving Canarian and Spanish food. For good local food in a humbler setting try the **Restaurante Plaza la Pila** (tel: 81 34 28) on the square of the same name.

Puerto de Santiago
In a resort dominated by bland international and British-orientated establishments the **Restaurant Casa Pancho** (tel:

The Isla Baja at Garachico is a justifiably popular spot

10 14 74) on Playa de la Arena is an oasis of high-quality local cooking.

Shopping
In Icod de los Vinos, the **Casa del Drago**, the **Salón Canario del Vino** and the **Casa del Vino** (all within a few yards of each other off Plaza de la Iglesia) offer a good range of Tenerife and Canarian wines and a selection of interesting Canarian comestibles.

Special Events
The **Romería de San Roque**, celebrated in Garachico in mid-August, is a colourful event and certainly the most interesting for visitors in this region.

THE SOUTH

The south of the island is almost permanently bathed in sunshine and its landscape is consequently harsh and arid. Thanks to the sunshine, and in spite of the aridity, tourism has taken such a firm hold here that over the past two decades the conurbation of Los Cristianos and Playa de las Américas has become one of the biggest resort areas in all Spain. While Los Cristianos still clings to vestiges of its Canarian heritage, Playa de las Américas is unencumbered by the past. It was created from scratch and so establishments like *Merrie England*, *The Knotted Hanky*, *Benny Hill's* and *The Yorkshire Pud* are the fantasy heritage and pastiche culture of this good-time boom town.

◆

LOS ABRIGOS
9 miles (15km) east of
Los Cristianos
This small fishing settlement is remarkable for the number of fish and seafood restaurants which crowd its harbour. It has an excellent reputation and draws locals, business executives and holiday-makers from miles around.
As you travel down the bumpy road to Los Abrigos notice the great swathe of green to your right. Amid such a barren landscape this is rather like seeing a mirage, but it is in fact the Golf del Sur complex (see **Sport**, page 82).

'Hell's Gorge' – a heavenly break from crowded beaches

◆◆◆
ADEJE/BARRANCO DEL INFIERNO
4 miles (6km) north of Playa de las Américas
The small unspoilt market town of Adeje sees many thousands of visitors each year. Only a fraction visit the town itself, the big attraction here is walking the Barranco del Infierno. Try to arrive early: firstly, so that the *barranco* isn't crammed full of fellow walkers, and secondly to find space to park your car – the walk up the very steep road to the entrance to the *barranco* is more tiring than the gorge itself! Despite its name ('Hell's Gorge') this abundant ravine is one of

the very few beauty spots in the desert landscape of southern Tenerife and the only *barranco* in the south with flowing water all year round. The goal is La Cascada, a 60-foot (20m) high waterfall, which the majority of people reach after 60 to 75 minutes walking. Then it's simply a case of following the path back. It is well marked and it is virtually impossible to get lost, particularly with the number of walkers around you. All you need are stout walking shoes (good trainers are fine) and a modicum of fitness. Take a sunhat and a drink along too. There are very few steep inclines and for much of the way the path is smooth.

On the first part of the walk notice the caves up above you, and those high on the other side of the valley. In these seemingly inaccessible eyries Guanche mummies were found. It's a sobering thought that in 1936

Journey to Atlantic depths with the Yellow Submarine

Franco's forces gave Hell's Gorge a new meaning by executing Republican prisoners here.

As the *barranco* sides start to close in on you the noise of rushing water becomes apparent and you will criss-cross a stream several times. After heavy rains the stream and waterfall are at their most spectacular, though the pathways and stepping stones usually remain clear so you shouldn't get your feet wet. Finally, mission completed, you can relax over a hearty meal in the **Restaurant Otelo** (see page 80) at the gorge entrance.

If you have the energy, walk to the bottom of the hill where, on the right, you will find the remains of the **Casa Fuerte**, a fortified mansion dating from the 16th century which was once owned by one of the most powerful families on the island. The **Iglesia de Santa Ursula**, opposite, dating from the 17th to 18th century, has a beautiful, painted coffered ceiling.

Los Cristianos port – home to pleasure and fishing craft

◆

COSTA DEL SILENCIO

7 miles (11km) southeast of Los Cristianos

So named before the airport was built close by, this rather barren area comprises the two major *urbanizaciones* (developments) of Costa del Silencio itself and Ten-Bel. The small fishing village of **Las Galletas**, with two small sand and shingle beaches, provides a little local interest, if not much colour. An authentic **Yellow Submarine** operates from Las Galletas, diving to 75 feet (25m), though despite its obvious novelty value it is difficult to justify the price of the trip for the views you get of modest Atlantic marine life (free buses from Playa de las Américas and Los Cristianos; tel: 73 00 13 for submarine reservations and information).

LOS CRISTIANOS

10 miles (15km) west of Aeropuerto Reina Sofía

Until the 1970s Los Cristianos was a humble tomato-shipping port. Since then it has exploded to become one of the most visited resorts in the Canary Islands. First impressions, based on the number of huge hotels and some fairly tacky tourist dives, may be that this is just another purpose-built resort, like neighbouring Playa de las Américas. But amid all the new development there are still signs of pre-tourism life. On the high street are shops which sell everyday items to local people; in the evenings the church square comes to life for the *paseo* and, despite the famous witty sign displayed by the El Bote *tapas* bar – *Se hable Español* (Spanish spoken here) – there are indeed plenty of bars where Spanish is still the *lingua franca*.

There is also a pleasing homogeneity to Los Cristianos that Playa de las Américas, spread among its various *urbanizaciones*, will never have. Compared to its neighbour, Los Cristianos draws a slightly older clientele which means fewer decibels and less rowdiness. The harbour is a busy and colourful focal point with a changing, picturesque mix of fishing boats, pleasure craft and ferries chugging to and from La Gomera.

There is a brown sandy beach which looks onto the harbour and on the other side of the harbour road is the newly created Playa de San Telmo, a brown-sand crescent relieving the crush on the old beach.

What to See Around Los Cristianos

It is only a five-minute bus or car journey to the centre of Los Cristianos to four major 'wildlife' attractions. All are served by free buses, departing from various points in Los Cristianos and Playa de las Américas.

◆◆◆
PARQUE ECOLÓGICO LAS AGUILAS DEL TEIDE (EAGLES OF TEIDE ECOLOGICAL PARK)
off the main road to Arona at km3 (tel: 75 30 01)
The island's newest attraction is a beautifully landscaped zoo park where an impressive display of free-flying eagles and condors is the main attraction. There is also a very colourful show of free-flying tropical birds. An elephant, penguins,

pigmy hippos, crocodiles, flamingos and pelicans are the other stars of the park – particularly at feeding times. Kids will also love the exciting bobsled run and the bumping-boats.
Open: daily, 09.00–18.00hrs.

◆◆
PARQUES EXÓTICOS (CACTUS AND ANIMAL PARK AND AMAZONIA)
just off exit 26 of the Autopista del Sur (tel: 79 54 24)
Cactus and Animal Park is a large cactus garden with a collection of small animals and birds. This is more interesting than it may sound with an informative leaflet to guide you round the many fascinating shapes and types of cactus here. If you have children in tow hurry along to the large walk-in cages where marmosets, squirrel-monkeys and other harmless small furry inmates scamper around you. There are also free-flying parrot aviaries.
Amazonia, on the same site, is a large dome encapsulating its very own rainforest. Here among dense foliage and exotic plants are more free-flying parrots, 100 hummingbirds (you'll have to keep your eyes peeled) and some 5,000 butterflies. Look out too for the large iguanas.
Open: daily, 10.00–19.00hrs.

◆
JARDINES DEL ATLÁNTICO BANANERA (ATLANTIC BANANA GARDEN)
follow signs from exit 26 of the Autopista del Sur (tel: 72 04 03)
Guided tours take visitors

around a working banana
plantation and farm, giving
general information on the
history and flora of the island
and explaining, among many
other things, how the water
percolates down from Mount
Teide and how it is used to
irrigate the barren fields of
southern Tenerife. The
emphasis is on education rather
than entertainment and, like the
landscape, can be rather dry.
Open: tours daily at 10.00, 11.30,
13.00, 15.30 and 16.15hrs.

◆
TENERIFE ZOO AND MONKEY PARK
*just off exit 26 of the Autopista del
Sur (tel: 75 13 68)*
Monkeys and primates are the
main attraction here, though
large cats and other animals
languish in some rather
uninspiring surroundings.
There's also a reptilarium and
camel rides on site (separate or

*A miniature rainforest in parched
southern Tenerife with thousands of
colourful inhabitants*

combined admission charges).
Open: daily, 09.30–18.00hrs.
End of Los Cristianos section

◆
EL MÉDANO
*13 miles (22km) east of
Los Cristianos*
This small charmless resort has
arguably the best, and certainly
the longest, of the southern
beaches with two sandy stretches
to either side of the landmark
Montaña Roja. They are largely
free from commercialism and
become quite wild the further
you go from the resort. Bring
your own sunshade and a
windbreak as the gusts here can
provide a real sand blasting.
This is a major reason why El
Médano has become one of the
Atlantic's windsurfing meccas
(see **Sport**, pages 83 and 110).

THE SOUTH

◆
PLAYA DE LAS AMÉRICAS

*10 miles (17km) west of
Aeropuerto Reina Sofía*

A boom town resort of
considerable proportions, Playa
de las Américas was built from
scratch in the late 1960s as a
home-from-home for north
European package holiday-
makers, and to this end it has
flourished remarkably well. As
long as you realise that it has
absolutely nothing in common
with native Tenerife, that you are
happy quaffing pints of British
beer and eating in
restaurants which proudly
proclaim 'no Spanish food
served here', then you will
probably love it.

There is no focus to Playa de las
Américas which is a sprawling
amorphous mass of *centro
commerciales* (shopping
centres) and *urbanizaciones*.

*The dark sands of Playa de las
Américas are soon covered with
bronzing bodies*

The most pleasant central spot
is the **Puerto Colón**, a smart
marina where yachts
congregate before crossing the
Atlantic and from where you can
take a cruise to see whales and
dolphins (see box, page 77).
Beaches are brown sand but
quite attractively laid out and
with all watersports facilities laid
on. Sheer numbers mean that
there is sometimes hardly room
to shake a towel. Many tourists
simply decamp to **Aguapark
Octopus**, at San Eugenio (just
off exit 29 of the Autopista del
Sur). This is a good family
waterpark with some exciting
water slides, good facilities for
little ones and a new dolphin
show. (*Open*: daily, from
10.00hrs, tel: 79 22 66.)

Whales and Dolphins

A colony of around 200 short-finned pilot whales lives just offshore between Punta de la Rasca (the southwest tip of the island) and San Juan. Bottle-nosed dolphins also frequent these waters and a whole flotilla of pleasure boats now cruises the waters off southwest Tenerife looking for these creatures. Many boats have special glass bottoms and glass-sided viewing compartments. Cruises depart from Playa de las Américas, Los Cristianos and also Los Gigantes. During migratory times other species of whale may also be spotted.

In the summer months, if you are lucky, flying fish, sharks and turtles may also be seen in these waters.

◆

VILAFLOR

13 miles (21km) northeast of Los Cristianos

Set on the slopes of Mount Teide, at an altitude of 3,809 feet (1,161m), Vilaflor is the highest village in the Canaries. It's quite an attractive place with a large if rather unkempt plaza and despite the hordes of Teide-trippers who pass through here, it is largely unspoiled.

If the weather ruins your day on the mountain console yourself by seeing the **Multivision** audio-visual show at the Parque Nacional del Teide at the Centro de Artesanía Chasna (see **Shopping**, page 88), just outside the village.

Clouds permitting, there's an excellent view down onto the village of Vilaflor and its agricultural environs from a *mirador* on the main road a little way further north.

Accommodation

There is no shortage of 3- or 4-star hotels in the conurbation of Los Cristianos/Playa de las Américas but many of them are block-booked by package tour operators and their atmosphere, facilities and activities reflect this.

Yet another misty day in cloud-swathed Vilaflor

Volcanic View

For the finest view of the whole south coast visit the **Mirador de la Centinela** on the C822 between San Miguel and Valle de San Lorenzo. Spread out below are the cones of dozens of extinct volcanoes.

THE SOUTH

The best bet, if you don't want a racy and over-sociable holiday, are apartments, set in their own grounds, away from the front and the *autopista*, preferably with a swimming pool. These are not too difficult to find in either Playa de las Américas or Los Cristianos.

The best hotel option in Los Cristianos is the 4-star **Arona Gran Hotel** (tel: 75 06 78), in a quiet location (but only a 5-minute walk from the centre), with very pleasant rooms, each with a sea-facing balcony, and a very attractive pool area.

In spite of its mass-market status Playa de las Américas has a surprising number of very prestigious hotels which insulate their guests from the rest of the resort. The most attractive of these is the beautiful Moorish-style 4-star **Jardín Tropical** in Urbanizacíon San Eugenio (tel: 75 01 00). Whitewashed galleries, arches and turrets reflect the island's proximity to North Africa. The gardens are splendid and the cooking is excellent (see **Restaurants**, pages 80–1). This is one of the island's most expensive hotels.

Children

With its beaches and various family attractions the south is a good place for children. But it can get very hot so keep them well protected. The best attractions for children are **Aguapark Octopus** and the **Parque Ecológico Las Aguilas del Teide**. Remember too that buses run from the south to **Loro Parque**, Puerto de la Cruz (see pages 50–1). Older children will enjoy whale and dolphin boat safaris too. Water-banana and water-sausage rides are available at Playa de las Américas.

Culture, Entertainment and Nightlife

A typical night out for young revellers in Playa de las Américas would probably include a video-bar and a karaoke contest followed by a high-energy disco, pausing only to take on beer and fast food. More discerning nightclubbers might like to try **Melody**, near the Pueblo Canario or **Prismas**, near the Tenerife Sol Hotel. The faint-hearted should avoid the Veronicas centres where behaviour is often excessive and trouble can (and does) break out. Los Cristianos is more restrained with fewer establishments of this type. Spanish or Canarian entertainment in the south is something of a novelty. The

Creative ways of cooling down at the Aguapark Octopus

Palace at San Eugenio stages a dinner show including South American Gauchos, Ballet Hawaii and *Ballet Español*. The lattor is an exciting hybrid of flamenco and ballet (oxit 29, Autopista del Sur, tel: 79 73 30 or 79 75 44 for reservations). The larger hotels also occasionally put on flamenco and Canarian folklore shows. A spectacular dinner show is provided at the Parque Ecológico Las Aquilas del Teide. **La Isla Mágica** is a mix of dance, magic and special effects set around an open-air stage and a Spanish galleon (Saturday to Monday 19.15–23.00hrs; tel: 75 30 01). The most popular show in the south is probably the *Medieval Night* at the mock Castillo San Miguel. Jousting knights, a medieval banquet and the famous 1960s soul band, the Drifters, provide a varied night of entertainment.
For a gimmick-free evening of great rhythm'n'blues with musicians from the American South, go to **Alabama's** (tel: 77 00 08), just off the *autopista* towards Granadilla de Abona. They also do good American 'soul food'.
You can gamble the night, and your money, away in the **Casino de las Américas** (*open*: 20.00–03.00hrs; tel: 79 37 12). It is owned by the same company that runs the Casino Taoro in Puerto de la Cruz and conforms to the same regulations (see pages 54–5).

Restaurants
Los Abrigos
The choice is wide and the quality is good in most, if not all, establishments, so browse before choosing. **La Lagostera** (tel: 17 03 02) occupies a prime position on the Paseo Marítimo,

THE SOUTH

service is efficient and the *menu del día* is very good value.

A simply decorated tipico *in Playa de las Américas*

Adeje
The **Restaurant Otelo** (tel: 78 03 74; closed Tuesdays), which occupies the entrance to the Barranco del Infierno, is a local attraction in its own right. Nonetheless it remains an unassuming and friendly place, serving excellent Canarian food at surprisingly low prices given its splendid site. It is famed for its chicken (basted in chilli and garlic before cooking) and rabbit, both of which come in generous portions.

Los Cristianos
Los Cristianos has a very good range of international and local eating houses and bars. You will even find an *arepera* bar (see box, page 99), **El Alazán** on Calle San Roque just behind El Bote (see below).
For *tapas* try **El Bote** on Calle El Cabezo, a characterful small

place where the bar is actually set into a small rowing boat. Directly opposite is the colourful, rustic-style **Rincón del Canario** (tel: 79 56 14) serving typical Canary dishes. Good local food and paella is served by the friendly staff of the **Restaurante Raymond** (tel: 79 04 52) at the far end of Calle General Franco.
Top international cooking (albeit at a price) is on offer at the long-established **El Sol** (tel: 70 05 69), Calle El Cabezo. For good quality Italian food try any one of the three branches of **Little Italy**. Fondues are the stars at the popular and attractive **Swiss Chalet** on Avenida de Suecia (tel: 79 14 26).

Playa de las Américas
For a special occasion the best place to eat is the award-winning **El Patio** restaurant at

the Jardín Tropical Hotel (tel: 75 01 00). Book a table outside on the patio and enjoy a menu which combines Andalucían and Canarian influences.

For considerably fewer pesetas, **El Dornajo**, Avenida Litoral (tel: 79 14 25), is one of the few places in Playa de las Américas where you can get good local food.

Vilaflor

The **Restaurante Sombrerito (Casa Chico)** on the main street is a good local establishment with an antique/junk shop attached and various bits of memorabilia decorating the dining area (tel: 70 90 52).

Shopping

There's little worth buying in the tawdry *centro commerciales* of the south. The open air **Torviscas Market** is held in front of the Hotel Esmeralda at Playa de las Américas (Thursdays and Saturdays 10.00–14.00hrs). It is the biggest on the island with 200 to 300 stalls and although much of the merchandise is of dubious quality, there is a good atmosphere. The same market, on a smaller scale, moves to Los Cristianos (near the Arona Gran Hotel), on Sunday 10.00–14.00hrs, and on Monday to Alcalá, also 10.00–14.00hrs. A mini-market (sometimes called the Hippy Market) is held every evening next to the Hotel Troya in Playa de las Américas. It sells toys, jewellery, leatherware and handicrafts. The **Centro de Artesanía Chasna** at the southern entrance to Vilaflor sells some beautiful traditional items from all over the island.

Special Events

The most colourful traditonal celebrations in the south are held in Vilaflor at **Corpus Christi** when the streets are decorated with sand pictures. *Carnaval* celebrations are boisterous but lack the panache of the north.

Sport
Diving

The **Coral-Sub Diving Centre** at the Ten-Bel Hotelpark is one of the best places in the south for both beginners and certified divers. Shipwreck dives, free diving with pilot whales and sighting of rays are promised. The centre is closed on Saturday afternoons and Sundays, for all of June and

It is well worth buying a sunhat in the hot south of the island

most of December (tel: 73 00 60 or 73 19 20).

Similar accredited dive centres are: Club Barracuda (tel: 78 07 25), Park Club Europe (tel: 75 27 08) and Las Palmeras (tel: 75 29 48) all at Playa de las Américas; Los Gigantes Diving Centre (fax: 10 04 31), Puerto de Los Gigantes.

Fishing
Various boats depart daily from Los Cristianos and Puerto Colón (Playa de las Américas) in search of deep sea and game fishing trophies.

Go-karting
The **Karting Club Tenerife** claims to be one of the best circuits in Europe and also features mini-bikes. It's on the Carretera del Chio, just off the Autopista del Sur, km66 Guaza, and will arrange a free pick-up from your hotel (tel: 73 07 03).

Waterskiing is expensive, but still popular in Playa de las Américas

Golf
The **Golf del Sur**, set within its own *urbanización* close to Los Abrigos, is a championship, 27-hole course which hosts the annual Tenerife Open which is part of the European PGA circuit. Consequently only golfers with a recognised handicap rating need apply (tel: 73 10 70).

If you are not up to this level, or you just fancy a cheaper warm-up round, try the **Golf Center Los Palos** where there is a 9-hole course, 1,000 yards (914m), plus driving range and practice putting and chipping areas (Carretera Guaza, Las Galletas, km7; tel: 73 00 80).

Horse Riding
The **Centro Hípico del Sur** gives tuition and undertakes daily excursions. It is located near the Go Karting on the Carretera de Buzanada km3, off Autopista del Sur, exit 26. *Open*: Tuesday to Sunday 08.00–22.00hrs (tel: 72 06 43).

Parapente (Paragliding)
Not to be confused with the
tame pastime of being hauled
along by a speed boat, this is
the altogether more risky
business of hurling yourself off a
cliff top on a parachute-like
wing. Flights high above
Tenerife in a dual-control
paraglider are on offer for a
very reasonable price with
several operators. Try
Parapente Club del Sur (tel: 78
13 57) or Parapente Tenerife
(tel: 52 42 63). Do check their
safety credentials and your
insurance policy first.

Squash
The **SurTen Squash Club** is
based at the Hotel Vulcano,
Playa de las Américas (tel: 79 20
35). The **Club de Tenis Las
Palmeras** (see **Tennis**, below)
also has two squash courts.

Ten-pin Bowling
Harley's American Superbowl
at Centro Commercial Fañabé,
Playa de las Américas offers 10
computerised Brunswick lanes
(tel: 71 30 40).

Tennis
TeniSur at San Eugenio (next to
the Aguapark) has three courts
for hire, with coaching and
tournaments (tel: 79 61 67). It
also offers badminton, mini-
golf, paddle tennis and a
bowling green. The **Club de
Tenis Las Palmeras** also stages
tournaments (every
Wednesday) and offers five
courts, tuition, mini-tennis for
children, and squash courts. It
is based in Playa de las
Américas at the Hotel Las
Palmeras (tel: 75 29 48).

*For a great sensation of low level
speed, go karting!*

Watersports
Waterskiing, jet skiing,
windsurfing (see below),
paragliding (at sea) and, for
kids, water bananas and water
sausages are all available at
Playa de las Américas.

Windsurfing
El Médano is definitely the place
for serious windsurfers (see
Sport, page 110) but there are
beginners' courses on offer
here, too. El Médano has
several schools and outlets for
board hire.
In Playa de las Américas
windsurfing boards may be
hired from opposite the Palm
Beach Club.

LA GOMERA

A short ride across the water from Los Cristianos, La Gomera is a small island measuring only 14 by 15 miles (23 by 25km) at its widest points. Its sides are rent by great gullies which affect journey times considerably. You won't be able to drive round it comfortably in a day and a minimum of two days is required to see the island properly.

First impressions are misleading. The barren landscape around the capital and ferry port of San Sebastián de la Gomera soon gives way to some of the most beautiful, luxuriant valleys in the

LA GOMERA

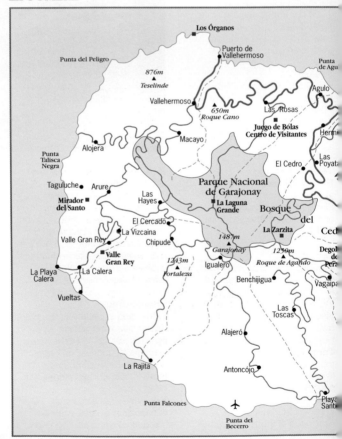

Canarian archipelago. At the centre of the island is a mist-covered rainforest, which has been designated a national park (Parque Nacional de Garajonay). From San Sebastián you can take one of two routes: the road north is a spectacular winding route calling at the island's most picturesque settlements. If you have only one day on the island head this way. The road south includes the island's two holiday destinations, the Hotel Tecina at Playa de Santiago and the Valle Gran Rey. Neither would even register on the southern Tenerife holiday development scale. The lack of tourism on La Gomera is at least half of the island's appeal, though things are destined to become a little busier. La Gomera, so long the only Canary Island without an airport, is about to join the aviation age – albeit only on an inter-island basis. With only one good beach on the whole island and an infrastructure and terrain unsuited to mass tourism, it is to be hoped that La Gomera will remain a shangri-la for many years to come.

◆◆◆
AGULO
15 miles (25 km) northwest of San Sebastián
The adjectives neat and tidy perfectly describe this small, pretty village of narrow cobbled streets. At its heart is a curiously designed grey-and-white-painted church with Moorish-style domes. Agulo's site is also picture-postcard perfect – enclosed in a natural amphitheatre of rocky cliffs, perched high above the sea with Tenerife's Mount Teide forming a majestic backdrop. After heavy rain waterfalls cascade down the cliffs.

◆◆
EL CERCADO/CHIPUDE
22 miles (37km) northwest of San Sebastián
El Cercado is famous for its rustic workshop homes where *alfarería* (pottery) is made from

The El Cercado pottery tradition dates back to Guanche times

the dark Gomeran earth without anything so sophisticated as a potter's wheel. From here there are fine views down to picturesque small farmsteads. Around the next bend is the neighbouring village of Chipude. With a total of four bars and a 16th-century church, this is comparatively a metropolis and enjoys a fine setting against the foot of the table-top mountain known as La Fortaleza (4,078 feet/1,243m).

◆◆◆
HERMIGUA
12 miles (20km) northwest of San Sebastián
The largest settlement on the island after San Sebastián,

Hermigua is a long straggling village clinging to the roadside above a beautiful lush valley of banana plantations. Vines are also grown here, strung on bamboo frames which hang diagonally across the hillsides like giant spiders' webs.
Visit the **Los Telares** craft centre to see the old house where girls weave traditional rugs on ancient looms. Close by is the 16th-century **Convento de Santo Domingo**.

◆◆
JUEGO DE BOLAS CENTRO DE VISITANTES (JUEGO DE BOLAS VISITORS' CENTRE)
20 miles (34km) northwest of San Sebastián (tel: 90 09 93)
This lively visitors' centre features well-labelled gardens illustrating island flora, a small museum of peasant life and craftspeople demonstrating basketry, weaving, pottery and woodworking. There are also displays on the Parque Nacional de Garajonay (see page 87). The road between the visitors' centre and the El Tabor bar (follow the track up, to the left) leads to a newly created *mirador* with spectacular views down to Agulo (see page 85) and across to Tenerife. The track at the end of the road is bumpy, but quite short and manageable in an ordinary car.
Open: Tuesday to Sunday 09.30–16.30hrs. (Craft workshops only open Tuesday to Friday.)

◆◆
LOS ÓRGANOS
Los Órganos (the 'organ pipes') is an extraordinary 650-foot-(200m) wide formation of

slender, tightly packed basalt columns. Some of these reach over 260 feet (80m) high and they do indeed resemble giant petrified church organ pipes. This natural wonder is located just off the north coast and may only be viewed from the sea.

Boats depart from Playa de Valle Gran Rey, Playa de Santiago and San Sebastián.

◆◆◆
PARQUE NATIONAL DE GARAJONAY (GARAJONAY NATIONAL PARK) ✔

This 10,000-acre (4,000ha) national park occupies the island's central high plateau and owes its protected status to its Canarian *Laurasilva* forest – the largest and most complete known example of the species left in the world. *Laurasilva* (a woodland of ferns, laurels and heath trees) thrives in damp conditions and much of the forest is cloaked in a veil of mist year-round. During the winter it is usually cold and damp, but in summer it dries to an extent where forest fires are a hazard. The highest point on the island, **El Alto de Garajonay** (Mount Garajonay) at 4,878 feet (1,487m), falls within the park and on a good day offers excellent views of the whole of La Gomera and the neighbouring islands.

◆◆
PLAYA DE SANTIAGO
20 miles (34km) southwest of San Sebastián
This would-be resort is in the infancy of tourism, with a handful of bars and restaurants lining its promenade and stony beach. At the far end is a small fishing port. Note the small fishermen's chapel decorated with model boats and seamen's knots and also the adjacent restaurant. Both are built right back into the rock face.

An excursion boat goes from the port to Los Órganos (see pages 86–7) and Valle Gran Rey (see

When the mists clear the Garajonay forest is a magical place

page 91). Above the beach is the **Hotel Tecina**. This is well worth a visit, even if you are not a resident, if only to see its gardens (see **Accommodation** and **Restaurants**, pages 92–3).

◆◆◆
LOS ROQUES
The main southern route from San Sebastián (TF713) passes a number of outstanding volcanic plug rock formations. The first, and most interesting, is the **Roque del Sombrero** (some 5 miles/8km from town) which actually resembles a pointed Chinese hat, peaking at 2,175 feet (663m).

After 10 miles (16km) there is a spectacular, windy, *mirador* at the pass known as the **Degollada de Peraza** (see **San Sebastián, Torre del Conde**, page 90). Looming above is the mightiest of the rocks, **Roque de Agando**, frighteningly large at an altitude of 4,101 feet (1,250m). As you return to San Sebastián along this road there is a magnificent view (weather permitting) of the town with Mount Teide in the distance.

◆◆
SAN SEBASTIÁN DE LA GOMERA
The island capital, San Sebastián, is famous above all for its associations with Christopher Colombus (in Spanish, Cristóbal Colón) who sailed from here in 1492 for the New World. The first reminders of this are the pavement tiles on the promenade which show the route of his voyage. They are hardly prominent though, and the town seems almost reluctant to celebrate Colombus – perhaps because he helped sell their ancestors into captivity. Today, San Sebastián is a pleasant small workaday place with a handful of historic buildings and, thanks to the ferry, plenty of activity – on the front at least – at either end of the day.

San Sebastián – a harbour known to Colombus and the **conquistadores**

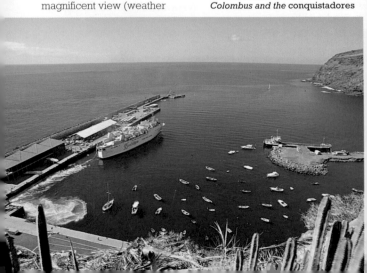

What to See in San Sebastián

Colombus was never here. The San Sebastián parador *is a glorious fake!*

◆
CASA COLÓN/CASA COLOMBINA (HOUSE OF COLOMBUS)
Calle del Medio (tel: 87 01 55)
The veracity of the Colombus connection is unproven and ironically this ancient house displays pre-Colombian ceramics, with old maps and models of Colombus' ships.
Open: Monday to Saturday 16.00–18.00hrs (subject to staff availability).

◆◆
IGLESIA DE LA ASUNCIÓN (CHURCH OF THE ASSUMPTION)
Calle del Medio
This ancient church is the one site in San Sebastián that we know Colombus visited. Records tell us he prayed here in 1492, even though most of the present church dates from the 16th century. It's a fine building, with some beautiful woodwork, notably the ceiling and the balcony above the entrance doors. Note too the decaying mural depicting the defence of the town against an English fleet in 1734.

◆◆◆
PARADOR CONDE DE LA GOMERA (PARADOR OF THE COUNT OF LA GOMERA)
Lomo de la Horca, directly above the town (turn right by the Iglesia de la Asunción)
Step into the beautiful *parador* courtyard and peeping out from behind the luxuriant plants you'll see portraits of Colombus, Beatriz de Bobadilla (see **Torre del Conde**, page 90) and other contemporary historical

worthies. Here, more than anywhere in San Sebastián, the spirit of this age is conjured up. So it comes as something of a disappointment to learn that it was built in 1973. It is a glorious reproduction of a typical aristocratic island mansion but has no historical pedigree at all. (See **Accommodation** and **Restaurants**, pages 92–3.)

◆

POZO DE COLÓN/POZO DE LA AGUADA (WELL OF COLOMBUS)

Calle del Medio (tel: 87 01 55)
An *aguada* is a station where ships took on water for long voyages and it is recorded that, among many others, the Spanish *conquistadores*, Pizzaro (conqueror of Peru) and Nuñez de la Balboa (the first European to set eyes on the Pacific Ocean)

Witty, modern art in the children's playground in Vallehermoso

both stopped here. It is perfectly logical (though unproven) that Colombus' men also took water from here to the New World and the notice next to the well states 'with this water America was baptised'.

The well, covered by a wooden lid, and tucked away in a pretty courtyard, is only accessible through the old Casa del Pozo de la Aguada (House of the Well), formerly the Custom House and now the tourist office. *Open*: Monday to Friday 08.30–14.00hrs and 16.30–18.00hrs; Saturday, Sunday 10.00hrs–noon.

◆◆

TORRE DEL CONDE (TOWER OF THE COUNT)

Parque de la Torre, next to the harbour front
This sturdy pink and white brick tower was built in 1447 by the first Count of La Gomera, Hernán Peraza the elder. His namesake son became the island tyrant and was killed by the Guanches at the **Degollada de Peraza** (see **Los Roques**, page 88).

Peraza's wife, the beautiful Beatriz de Bobadilla (once the mistress of King Ferdinand of Spain) was also notorious for her brutality. She fled here and subsequently helped put down the rebellion. She is also said to have entertained Colombus, and went on to marry Alonso de Lugo, the conqueror of Tenerife. In subsequent years the tower was used for storing riches from the New World *en route* to Spain. Its interior is now very fragile and it has been closed to visitors for many years.

End of San Sebastián section

◆◆◆
VALLE GRAN REY
31 miles (52km) west of San Sebastián

The origin of the name, which means Valley of the Great King, goes back to Guanche times, and its majesty remains undiminished by the passing of

Views into the Valle Gran Rey are still fit for a king

time. There is only one road leading into and out of the valley. Towards the bottom the views to the emerald green slopes on the far side are breathtaking, with row upon row of little white houses perched precariously on steep terraces climbing high up the slopes. At the bottom, the road splits – left to the port, right to **La Playa Calera**. The latter is the only sandy beach on the island and is showing signs of small-scale development. The pretty village of **La Calera** lies behind the resort, back up the hill.
En route to the Valle Gran Rey stop at the **Mirador del Santo** at Arure (6 miles/10km north of La Calera). It is one of the finest viewpoints on the island.

El Silbo – **Language without Words**

Due to the communications difficulties imposed by the landscape, the Gomerans have developed a unique language known as *el silbo* (the whistle). This is far more than mere whistling, with real modulation, vocabulary and, most importantly, stentorian volume. It is said that some *silbadores* can communicate from up to 3 miles (5km) away. But with the advent of telecommunications and the decline of the traditional way of life, practitioners are becoming rare. The only place where you will definitely see it now is at Las Rosas restaurant (see **Restaurants**, page 93).

◆◆◆
VALLEHERMOSO
25 miles (42km) northwest of San Sebastián
This compact village hugging

the valley side is a fine sight, particularly when approached from the TF112 to the north. At the entrance to Vallehermoso is a particularly artistic children's playground. The giant sculpture of three curvaceous women with head-dresses would grace many a modern art museum. Vallehermoso has a lively centre with two bustling *tapas* bars, and old houses rise up to the church. Just above the village is the **Roque Cano** (Dog Rock) so named because of its resemblance to a canine tooth, which reaches some 2,132 feet (650m) into the sky.

Accommodation

La Gomera has two of the best hotels in the Canary Islands. The **Parador** (see **San Sebastián**, pages 89–90) is recognised as one of the finest small *paradores* in Spanish territory and its bedrooms and public areas are in complete harmony with its Colombian atmosphere. Its gardens are pretty and its swimming pool overlooks the harbour. There are only 42 rooms so book well ahead (tel: 87 11 00).

The **Hotel Tecina** (tel: 89 50 50) is every bit as impressive. The setting, on the cliff edge above Playa de Santiago, basking in the sunniest part of the island, with Teide looming large, is magnificent. The hotel grounds resemble an ideal Canarian village, with individual houses designed in the local style, providing accommodation on either ground or first floor. The

One of the great sights on La Gomera is, ironically, Mount Teide, here floating serenely above Agulo

the island in an atmospheric dark-wood dining room (tel: 87 11 00). However, it is difficult to beat the romantic balcony setting of the **Hotel Tecina International Restaurant** (tel: 89 50 50).

Las Rosas restaurant (at Las Rosas) also enjoys a stunning setting, perched precariously on the edge of a ravine, with magnificent 180-degree views. The food is typically Canarian, but tailored to coach parties who come here to witness the amazing *el silbo* (see box, page 91). *Open*: noon–15.00hrs only (tel: 80 09 16).

In San Sebastián try the attractive **Marqués de Oristano**, Calle del Medio (tel: 87 00 22).

gardens are a showcase of indigenous and exotic flora, perfectly manicured and labelled, with a beautiful swimming pool area.

There are very few mid-range hotels in La Gomera so if you can't get into either of these (or don't fancy their tarrifs) go native and pick up a *turismo rural* brochure from the tourist office. This details many charming houses and apartments for rent in Agulo, Hermigua and Vallehermosa. The **Apartmentos Los Telares** (tel: 88 07 81) and **Apartmentos La Casa Creativa** (tel: 88 10 23), both at Hermigua, are particularly pleasant.

Restaurants

The **Parador** serves the best food (Spanish and Canarian) on

Sport

Walking is the most strenuous pastime on the island. The trails within the Parque Nacional de Garajonay are very popular. The information centre at Juego de Bolas has walking maps and there is another centre at Laguna Grande. On Fridays, walking tours depart from here. Reservations are essential (tel: 80 09 93, Juego de Bolas office). Guided walking tours may also be organised through the travel agency inside the Hotel Tecina.

Special Events

The most important date in the Gomeran calendar is the first Monday of October when the festival of the Virgin of Guadalupe is celebrated in San Sebastián.

Peace and Quiet

*Wildlife and Countryside
on Tenerife
by Paul Sterry*

Tenerife is a perfect destination for any traveller seeking a relaxing holiday but eager to pursue an interest in natural history as well. Although it lies off the coast of north Africa, the island's subtropical climate is tempered by the cool seas which bathe it. The oceanic location of Tenerife, and indeed the other islands in the Canaries, has also brought about some extraordinary developments in the wildlife which has evolved in isolation. Botanists in particular are in their element with the vast majority of the islands floral list comprising endemic plants, that is flowers that are found nowhere else in the world. The bird list, although comparatively short, also includes a few endemic species along with several which are difficult to see anywhere else in Europe.

Apart from its climate and geographical location, two other factors affect the wildlife and vegetation of Tenerife. Dominated by snow-capped

The summer slopes of Mount Teide glow bright with giant bugloss

Mount Teide, the island has a large altitudinal range which in itself has contributed to the diversity of plant and animal life. The influence of man, felt most in the last two hundred years, has had a distinctly negative effect on the native wildlife: forest clearance, agriculture and coastal development are the areas in which human impact is most obvious. Nevertheless, the visitor can still find stunning coastal scenery, pockets of native laurel forest and, of course, the stunning and unspoilt scenery of Mount Teide.

Mount Teide

Protected by national park status within the Parque Nacional del Teide, the extinct volcano of Mount Teide and its lower slopes undoubtedly harbour the scenic and wildlife highlights of any visit to Tenerife. The snow-capped summit, which at 12,198 feet (3,718m) is not only the highest mountain in the Canaries but also in Spain, can be seen from almost anywhere on the island. The views are stunning at Parador Nacional de las Cañadas and there is an information centre at El Portillo; the summit

PEACE AND QUIET

Great spotted woodpeckers may be seen on the forested lower slopes of Mount Teide

The Teno Mountains

Situated in the northwest of Tenerife, the Teno Mountains have some of the most dramatic coastal scenery on the island with sheer cliffs plunging to the raging seas below. Those at El Fraille are spectacular and easily accessible, also harbouring some of the richest areas of endemic plants. As elsewhere in the islands, the various species of endemic spurges such as *Euphorbia canariensis* are among the most conspicuous members of the

can reached on foot or by cable car (see pages 60–1).

The range of plants found on Mount Teide is huge but without doubt the most impressive of these is the endemic bugloss *Echium wildpretii*, huge red spikes which dot the landscape. Birdwatchers should scan the skies above for plain swifts while the open slopes are home to Berthelot's pipits and trumpeter finches. Visitors with their own cars may like to break the descent by stopping among the forests of Canary pines on the lower slopes. Here you may find blue chaffinches, canaries and great spotted woodpeckers if you are lucky.

The Canary

Although best known to most people as a familiar cage bird, the canary lives wild on these eponymous islands and is common and widespread on Tenerife; it also occurs on Madeira and in the Azores. Canaries can be found in all manner of different habitats from pine forests to agricultural land. They are primarily seed-eaters and spend much of their time foraging on the ground but at other times they often perch on the tops of tall trees. The canary is, of course, renowned for the quality of the male's song which can be heard at almost any time of the year. Although often sung from a perch, birds will sometimes perform fluttering, circular song-flights. Outside the breeding season, the species usually gathers in large flocks which make an impressive sight and sound in flight.

plant community. Although cactus-like, they are unrelated to the New World plants; their similar appearances have evolved in response to the same environmental factor, namely the need to conserve water.

Anaga Mountains

Rising to an altitude of some 3,280 feet (1,000m), the Anaga mountains dominate the northeastern peninsula of Tenerife. Winding roads from La Laguna to Las Mercedes lead through this, the most accessible of the remaining areas of native laurel forest, the wooded slopes being home to two of the Canaries' most threatened endemic birds. Visitors should take advantage of viewpoints along the way and stop to look for rare and endangered Bolle's and laurel pigeons, both of which occur here. Canaries and Canary firecrests may be found by exploring the interior of the ancient forest itself which also harbours many interesting plants.

Huge forests of Canary pine stretch along the Cumbre Dorsal. They harbour some of the island's more interesting birds

Endemic Plants

In the Canaries as a whole, a staggering 2,000 or so species of native plants can be found, most of which are endemic to the islands. Of these, the majority can be found on Tenerife and a trip here can be a botanical experience unrivalled in any other part of Europe. The number of plant species found here reflects the range of habitats encountered and the altitudinal range of the island, while the high proportion of endemics is a consequence of 20 million years or so of isolation from mainland Africa. At the highest altitudes on Tenerife, vegetation is limited to ground cover of small shrubs but at slightly lower levels open pine forests predominate. Lower still, where clouds and mist prevail for lengthy periods, evergreen forests comprising laurel and other species would be the dominant vegetation if so much of it had not been cleared by man. Around the coasts, a dense scrub mixture including some Mediterranean plants, along with endemic succulent species of spurge and *Aeonium*, and members of the daisy family (*Compositae*) predominates.

PEACE AND QUIET

Seabirds

The seas surrounding Tenerife are full of marine life and provide excellent feeding for numerous seabirds. Some of these are seasonal, non-breeding visitors to the region but other species are resident and breed on inaccessible and precipitous cliffs or on offshore islets. Species to look out for include Cory's shearwater, a comparatively large, brownish seabird which flies on stiffly held wings; its diminutive relative, the little shearwater, also occurs in these waters. The all-dark Bulwer's petrel is a blue-riband bird for many birdwatchers and smaller still are the European and Madeiran storm-petrels, tiny dark birds with conspicuous white rumps. Headlands and promontories almost anywhere around the island may afford good views of seabirds, especially during periods of onshore winds or at dusk. An alternative option is to take the ferry to La Gomera which will often provide closer sightings of the birds.

Look out for Cory's shearwater on or near sheer cliffs. They visit their cliffside burrow nests at dusk, but can be seen flying offshore during the daytime

El Médano

By way of a change from the high altitude scenery and vegetation of Mount Teide and the forests of Anaga, visitors should head for the south of the island. Near El Médano and Los Cristianos can be found dry, semi-desert scenery and dune formations, the vegetation dominated by cactus-like species of endemic spurges and drought-loving euphorbias; and the tamarisk (*Tamarix canariensis*) can be seen here too, another entirely endemic species.

The birdlife comprises dry-country species including Barbary partridge, Berthelot's pipit and trumpeter finch. A good starting point for exploring the area is Las Galletas. Remember to take plenty of water and a hat to provide shade.

Practical

This section includes information on food, drink, shopping, accommodation, nightlife, tight budget, special events, etc

FOOD AND DRINK

Real Canarian food is tasty, fresh and filling, though rarely glamorous. In the resorts of the south it is usually easier to find a 'real British pub' or a fast-food restaurant than a Canarian *típico* (typical native restaurant) but elsewhere on the island it's not too difficult. A *típico* is distinguished by a relatively short menu of soups, stews and grilled fish dishes. The best alternative, if you want to sample food which the locals eat, is to find a place serving *tapas*. This is the Spanish custom of serving small portions of local food, usually in bars and cafés. *Tapas* bars are quite thin on the ground in the tourist centres. Informal restaurant-bars serving *tapas* are sometimes known as *tascas*.

Eating out is relatively inexpensive. In the resorts competition tends to keep prices down (though this may be at the expense of quality), whereas in the villages eating out is generally priced for the locals. If you don't mind fairly basic amenities, a menu with little choice, and you can manage a few words of Spanish,

the latter is nearly always better value. Canarian portions are usually large.

Eating out is nearly always an informal occasion with reservations only required at a handful of the most popular restaurants. Children are welcome, indeed encouraged, virtually everywhere.

Local Cuisine

Canarian cuisine is essentially peasant and fishermen's food. Meat only features as part of a stew (usually pork, veal or rabbit) and steaks, generally

---

Areperas

An *arepera* is just an ordinary café-bar/bar-restaurant, serving *arepas*. Look for the word *arepera* incorporated (often inconspicuously) into the restaurant sign. *Arepas* are delicious small Venezuelan sandwiches, made from semolina flour and deep fried. Fillings include *pollo* (chicken), *cerdo* (cold roast pork), *carne* (beef) and *atún salpicón* (tuna in a spicy sauce). A red pepper sauce (not as hot as *mojo picón*, see page 100) and a cool green *aguacate* (avocado) sauce are also offered separately.

FOOD AND DRINK

imported from Spain or South America, are for tourists only. Soups and stews are the most typical Canarian meals. *Potaje* comprises just vegetables and may be a stew or a soup; meat is added to make *rancho canario* soup. *Puchero*, generally a main course, is a combination of several different vegetables and boiled pork. All these dishes are flavoured differently with herbs such as thyme, saffron (which turns the boiled potatoes bright yellow), marjoram, parsley and particularly cumin and coriander, but basic ingredients are similar. That Guanche staple, *gofio* (maizemeal, toasted and milled), once eaten as a bread, is still used to thicken stews. Another common stew is *garbanzo compuesto* (chickpea stew with meat), often available as a *tapas* dish.

A favourite casserole on Tenerife is *conejo con salmorejo* (rabbit in sauce).

Chicken is usually simply

Jamón de serrano and cheese are favourite tapas *items in real Canarian bars*

roasted or fried but sometimes it is smothered in garlic and chilli sauce then roasted or deep fried to acquire a mouth-watering crispy coating.

Fresh fish is always on the menu and seaside restaurants can offer a bewildering list (although it's rarely the case that everything on the menu is available). The method of cooking is usually plain – either boiled, fried or grilled (often on a barbecue). The traditional accompaniment to most Canarian meals is salad and *papas arrugadas* – small new-style potatoes, boiled in their jackets in very salty water. On the table will be placed two cold olive oil-based sauces, red *mojo picón* (piquant sauce) and *mojo verde* (green sauce). The latter is a cool parsley and coriander sauce, perfect with fish, the former is a spicy chilli and paprika mix, generally poured over potatoes and red meat.

The most famous Canarian dessert is *bienmesabe*, a concoction of almonds, sugar, sponge cake, eggs and lemon. It is delicious with cream or ice cream. Don't turn your nose up at the ubiquitous *flan* (a cooked milk dessert, like crème-caramel). In any good local restaurant this will be home-made and a source of some pride to the maker.

Drinks

Since 1984 when strict quality rules were drawn up by the island's wine producers, Tenerife has enjoyed a renaissance in the quality and sales of its wines. The best places to try the island wines are Icod de los Vinos, Tacoronte and the Casa del Vino La Baranda at El Sauzal. As an introduction try one of the styles of Viña Norte. Unfortunately, due to the small scale nature of production, prices cannot compete with wines from the Spanish mainland so the latter are usually the only wines on offer in restaurants. Canarian after-dinner drinks include *mistel* (a dessert wine), *parra* (an *aguardiente* brandy) and the sweeter, ubiquitous *Ronmiel* (honey-rum). The latter is actually distilled sap from the palm tree, and is gathered in La Gomera. The resultant cocktail is a pleasant smooth orange-tasting drink.

(For tips on coffee and beer see **How to be a Local**, page 105.)

Al fresco dining at Playa de las Américas

SHOPPING

The first lesson to learn is to take tax-free and duty-free signs with a pinch of salt. The luxury goods on which favourable tax rates apply are typically electrical items, cameras, calculators, jewellery, perfume, leather goods, tobacco and spirits. The last two items are certainly bargains but elsewhere there is often little to choose between retailers and airport duty-free shop prices. Be aware also that in 1997 taxes and duties on these goods may increase in line with EU directives.

The best place for duty-free shopping is Santa Cruz which is also known for its Indian bazaars, where you may be able to haggle for goods.

La Orotava is the craft centre of the island and should satisfy all your handicraft requirements. Look out for *rosetas* (lace doilies), *calados* (drawn threadwork embroidery used for decorating table linen) and *ristra* (basketware made from palm fronds).

The speciality of La Gomera is the Guanche-style pottery.

Markets

The island's best market is the Nuestra Señora de África at Santa Cruz. This is *the* place to buy fresh fruit and vegetables. On Sundays its bustling *rastro* (flea market) has a strong African presence. The Torviscas markets in the southern resorts are also worth a look for cheap T-shirts and jewellery.

Island Produce

Tenerife consumables which make interesting presents or tasty souvenirs include *mojo* sauces (see pages 99 and 100) in small gift packs, and local wines. Cigars are hand-rolled at several places and compare favourably to Cuban cigars. A bunch of strelitzias is an exotic way of saying it with flowers. Florists will box these for you so that they may go straight into the aircraft hold (or you can buy them from street sellers, unboxed, at half the price). These flowers are hardy travellers and will last for a good number of weeks once cut.

Santa Cruz isn't all modern malls and international stores

ACCOMMODATION

Typical Tenerife apartment accommodation at Los Gigantes

The vast majority of tourist accommodation on Tenerife is in 3- and 4-star Mediterranean and international-style hotels which have been built over the last 20 years to cater for package holiday-makers. Standards are similar over the whole island though the hotels of the south are generally newer and therefore generally have better facilities than those in the north. There is not a large pool of private accommodation for independent travellers but recent *turismo rural* initiatives have improved the chances of finding comfortable characterful accommodation away from the packaged crowds. La Gomera is particularly good in this respect. Ask the tourist office to send you a list before you depart.

All tourist offices will assist with accommodation lists and general advice but they do not provide a booking service. The year-round popularity of Tenerife and the comparative scarcity of accommodation on La Gomera means that it is always a good idea to book in advance wherever you intend staying.

Paradores

Paradores are Spanish state-run hotels, set up to provide top-quality local-style lodgings in regions where accommodation was scarce. La Gomera's mock-colonial Conde de la La Gomera is one of the finest in the whole chain while in Tenerife the Cañadas del Teide has recently been refurbished.

For central bookings contact Paradores de España, Central de Reservas, Calle Requena 3, 28013 Madrid (tel: 01-559 00 69; fax 01-559 32 33). In the UK contact Keytel International, 402 Edgware Road, London W2 1ED (0171 402 8182). Enquire at the Spanish Tourist Office in other countries.

Self-catering

Aparthotels (hotel apartments) feature rooms with their own kitchen facilities, yet retain most of the other trappings of an ordinary hotel. These are popular in the larger resorts. Self-catering bungalows and apartments are a popular holiday choice and are usually grouped together in *urbanizaciones*.

CULTURE, ENTERTAINMENT AND NIGHTLIFE

You're never short on quantity of entertainment in the modern resorts of the south but the quality and variety is lacking. It is basically a choice between international cabaret shows and grotesque home-from-home fun pubs. If you're 18 to 30 in age or mentality, in Playa de las Américas there's a video-bar and karaoke machine every few yards. If you want something more, and you are looking for something that is locally inspired, you will have a long search.

Only in Puerto de la Cruz is there a choice of bars where you can hear local musicians. These are often lively affairs with pulsating Latin rhythms and infectious songs. The audience is often encouraged to join in too, even if only shaking the maracas or singing along.

For highbrow nightlife you'll have to go to Santa Cruz (see pages 27–8). The free magazine *Tenerife Holiday Gazette* has a useful What's On section covering everything from classical to karaoke.

Flamenco

Although it has nothing do with the Canaries, flamenco shows are regularly staged by the top hotels, and a good flamenco troupe is always worth seeing. Look too for advertisements in bars and restaurants.

Folklore

Canarian folklore shows are gentle but enjoyable family affairs with large groups of young, and not so young, musicians accompanying a dance troupe in traditional costume. The rhythms are generally Spanish, though lacking the passion of the flamenco, and instruments include guitars, flutes and the small ukulele-like *timple*. There's only one folklore show staged regularly on Tenerife, and that is at the Hotel Tigaiga in Puerto de la Cruz, every Sunday morning (see page 55). Larger hotels throughout the island stage occasional folklore nights.

Neon nightlife in Playa de las Américas – certainly not for the faint-hearted!

WEATHER AND WHEN TO GO

The combination of trade winds and a very high mountain ensures that there is a very clear weather distinction between the north and the south of Tenerife. In winter the north can be overcast and wet for days on end, particularly during November and continuing through January. The only consolation is that it is unlikely to be cold, averaging around 64°F (18°C). Meanwhile the south bathes in sunshine almost all year round (there is the occasional cloudy day and the very odd spell of rain). As it is only just over an hour's drive from Puerto de la Cruz to Los Cristianos sun-starved holiday-makers in the north can quickly escape to a sunny clime.
In the summer too much heat is the only problem in the south, though temperatures rarely get unbearable, whereas the north is just about right.
The high season, when hotel prices are at their peak, is between November and April, reflecting the northern European desire to escape the winter. Prices fall from May through October and some establishments also offer a small extra discount during May and June. Increasingly, however, the season is becoming all year round.
La Gomera also has a north–south divide, though as more people come here to walk than to sunbathe an overcast day is often regarded as good weather. The pattern is similar to Tenerife. The sunniest part of the island is the south. The central part of the island is often covered in a thick mist and the north is sunny in summer, overcast in winter.
Accommodation charges vary little, if at all, throughout the year.

HOW TO BE A LOCAL

If you want to get straight into the thick of Canarian local life just walk into any busy café-bar. Order a *café solo* (which is like an expresso) or a *cortado* which is an expresso with a drop of milk. Only tourists order the milky white *café con leche*. Beware, most *cortados* have a slug of condensed milk and/or sugar included. To avoid this ask for a *cortado natural*. If you want a beer, order a *caña* (a small draft beer) or a *Dorada*, the brand name of the excellent island brew.
Most Canarians are convivial and friendly when visitors enter their midst, so try and chip into the conversation. Even if

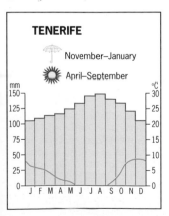

TENERIFE

November–January

April–September

mm / °C chart, x-axis: J F M A M J J A S O N D

A Santa Cruz local

friends or family there.)

In remoter parts of the island and particularly on La Gomera locals may well appreciate a lift so if you are driving past an old man walking along the road with his tools or bags, returning home from the fields, stop and offer (women should not pick up strangers). If you're lucky you may well be invited into their home for a glass of local wine.

Remember, older Canarians are still very traditional and old-world courtesies (shaking hands, for example) are always observed. Similarly you should never enter a church without being modestly covered. Shorts are generally acceptable but men without shirts and women wearing halter-neck tops or plunging necklines may well give offence.

Remember too that Canarians still generally observe the *siesta*, closing down for a nap between 13.00 and 16.00hrs. Avoid sightseeing, or even strolling around towns and villages during the siesta, as they turn into ghost towns. After the siesta comes the *paseo*, the early evening stroll, the time to see, be seen and enjoy a drink and some *tapas*.

CHILDREN

Because of its sand and sunshine the south is the best place for a family holiday on Tenerife. The north is more attuned to adults, while La Gomera really is not geared for children.

Wherever you go, you will find that the Canarians, like the Spanish, love children.

your Spanish isn't good, there is usually someone who speaks some English. And, despite the obvious effects of tourism on the island you don't have to move too far away from the resorts before a Spanish phrase book comes in handy. As always it's best to avoid discussing politics and never express any admiration for mainland Spain! (By the same token it is not wise to critisise Spain either – your fellow conversants may well have

Daytime Activities

You can choose your mount from camel or donkey at El Tanque (near Garachico) while a different type of safari, spotting whales and dolphins from boat trips in the south, may well appeal to older children (see box, page 77). Tenerife has four wildlife parks. The biggest and best is the Florida-style **Loro Parque**, at Puerto de la Cruz, but **Aguilas del Teide**, near Los Cristianos, is also very good. Near by you can also try **Parques Exóticos** and **Tenerife Zoo and Monkey Park**.

For simply messing about in the water **Aguapark Octopus** at Playa de las Américas is excellent, while down at the beach, water bananas and 'ringos' (inflatables pulled behind a speedboat) splash along, and there are pedaloes for hire.

Night-time Activities

Castillo de San Miguel, east of Playa de las Americas, provides a medieval jousting show for all the family. Folklore and flamenco shows will also probably go down well with older children. The colour, costumes, fireworks and general excitement of *Carnaval* means that this can be a marvellous time to bring slightly older children to the island. You will never have any trouble taking children or babies into local restaurants or café-bars. Indeed they will usually be welcomed with open arms. Fussy eaters are well catered for with myriad tourist restaurants to choose from. Larger hotels provide a baby-listening service and should be able to recommend local, reliable babysitters.

TIGHT BUDGET

● If you're not too concerned about the type or location of hotel book your holiday as late as possible.

● Book a flight only, then contact the tourist office in the resort for a list of private accommodation offering rooms only, or camp (but you must book ahead).

● The *menú del día* (menu of the day) always provides the cheapest two- or three-course meal and, pound for pound, is the best value way of filling up. The most expensive way is *tapas*. The *menú del día* is available at both lunchtime and in the evenings.

● Drinks usually cost more in tourist bars (but do look out for special '2 for 1', 'happy hour' offers). Ask for a *caña* (small draft beer) or, as a tourist, you may automatically be given a large draft beer. There is little price difference between a small bottle of local beer and draft.

● As a general rule avoid organised excursions. Car hire is relatively cheap, public transport is very cheap, and you see places at a more relaxed pace on your own. Evening shows are normally the same price for groups and individuals.

● Despite advice to the contrary the airport duty free shop is actually cheaper on some items of alcohol. The choice is wider in local supermarkets.

● Go walking. The scenery is magnificent in the north of the island and on La Gomera.

SPECIAL EVENTS

All the following traditional celebrations include a procession, which is secular (marching bands and fancy costumes) or religious, depending upon the event. Sometimes it is a combination of both. The streets come alive with food and drink vendors and musical and folk events. Fireworks often round off the revelries. In addition to the following list are several *patronal* festivals, celebrating local saints.

5 January: The *Cabalgata de los Reyes Magos* (The Procession of the Three Kings) is celebrated best in Santa Cruz.

Late February/Early March: *Carnaval* (Carnival) is by far the biggest event of the year (see pages 28 and 109–10).

Romería time at Santa Cruz with a local folk group

Easter: *Semana Santa* (Holy Week) is celebrated all over the island. The best procession is in La Laguna.

May: The *Fiestas de Primavera* (Spring Festivals) in Santa Cruz focus on the performing arts and folklore events.

June: Corpus Christi is the most colourful time of year after *Carnaval*, particularly in La Orotava, La Laguna and Vilaflor. Following on from this are the *romerías*. Although the word means pilgrimage, the celebrations are also of a secular nature, akin to an agricultural carnival and the festivities include lively processions of decorated carts pulled by bullocks.

July: around the middle of the month Santa Cruz celebrates the *Fiesta de la Virgen del Carmen*, with nautical festivities, and Puerto de la Cruz stages the *Fiestas del Gran Poder de Dios*.

14–15 August: The most important pilgrimage in the Canary Islands draws tens of thousands to Candelaria to pay tribute to the *Virgen de la Candelaria* (see pages 25–7).

16 August: The *Romería de San Roque* in Garachico is a colourful event.

25 August: Santa Cruz celebrates the defeat of Admiral Nelson in 1797 (see **Background**, box, page 13).

September: The *Fiestas del Santísimo Cristo*, held in La Laguna and Tacoronte, turn into something of a wine harvest festival.

For precise dates and further details (if available) contact the nearest tourist office.

Carnaval

Carnaval is the biggest, costliest, most frenzied and eagerly awaited event on the island each year. It takes months to make some of the costumes and the floats too are often works of art. Celebrations go on for two hedonistic weeks with a programme of nightly outdoor dancing, usually to the hottest Latin American dance bands, fancy dress and drag competitions. Stalls selling *cubata* (rum and coke), *churros*

The **timple** *is a special Canarian instrument, between guitar and ukelele*

(a type of Spanish doughnut) and *pinchitos* (kebabs) are found everywhere.

The highlight of course is the main procession. Comparison with the famous Río de Janeiro carnival is obvious, and perhaps not surprising given the number of *Canarios* who have emigrated to South America. The drummers beat out pulsating Latin rhythms while the carnival queens stand proud on top of the procession floats in their magnificent dresses and feathered headdresses. The troupes alongside the floats, also dressed-to-kill in glitter, feathers and often little else, rumba and samba along the whole procession route. Alongside them are drag queens, Charlie Chaplin and Fidel Castro look-alikes plus a multitude of fancy-dressed children.

You will probably see many strange sights during *Carnaval* but none so strange as the final ceremony, known as the Burial of the Sardine. A 24 to 30-foot-(8 to 10m) long cardboard-and-papier-mâché sardine is dragged to the harbour or the main square accompanied by mourners. The latter are invariably men dressed in black drag, theatrically weeping and wailing. At the appointed spot, fireworks inside the sardine are set off and it literally blows itself apart. A grand firework display then takes place.

The best places to catch *Carnaval* are Santa Cruz and Puerto de la Cruz (during which time accommodation becomes fully booked and it is difficult to get a good night's sleep in the central area). Dates vary, check with the tourist office in Santa Cruz. *Carnaval* begins in Santa Cruz, ending on Ash Wednesday, then fans out to the rest of Tenerife and the other Canary Islands.

SPORT

Tenerife is not an important sporting destination and only the thrill-seeking windsurfers of El Médano come here specifically for the island conditions. Clear, warm waters and a balmy winter climate mean that Tenerife is a good year-round venue for all sporting types.

Watersports

Only the south of the island is suitable for watersports, and here **windsurfing** is king. Jetskiing and waterskiing are mostly confined to Playa de las Américas. **Diving** is also quite popular (see pages 81–2).

Land Sports

Many large hotels have their own tennis courts, or at least have arrangements with other

El Médano is the venue for the annual windsurfing World Cup

a recognised handicap (see page 82). In the north try the Golf Tenerife El Peñon at Tacoronte (tel: 25 02 40/25 02 30) which has 18 holes, 5,700 yards (5,200m). Mountain bikes are available for hire in the major resorts, or you could try go-karting (see page 82).

Spectator Sports
Tinerfeños, like the Spanish, are passionate about **football**. CD Tenerife, whose home ground is in Santa Cruz, play in the Spanish First Division and so play host to the likes of Barcelona and Real Madrid. Matches are usually on a Saturday evening or a Sunday. The traditional Canarian fighting sport of **wrestling** (***Lucha Canaria***) is likely to appeal to fans of Japanese sumo wrestling. The basic objective is to throw your opponent to the ground, but as in sumo, there are many gentlemanly rituals to be observed.

hotels or *urbanizaciones* close by. There are also centres where tournaments are regularly held for visitors (see page 83).
There are three **golf** courses on the island, but the best, Golf del Sur, is only open to players with

The Golf del Sur, a splash of cool green in the sun-baked south

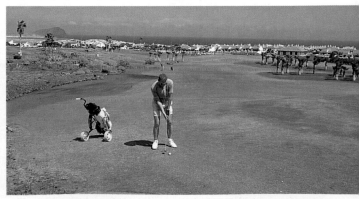

Directory

This section contains day-to-day information, including travel, health, documentation, money matters and language tips

Contents

Arriving

By Air

Tenerife has two international airports. Tenerife South (Reina Sofia) is the main airport and is used for charter flights. Tenerife North (Los Rodeos) is only used for scheduled and inter-island flights. The airport on La Gomera is scheduled to be open for inter-island flights during 1997.

By Sea

The only major sea route is from mainland Spain. Ships sail from Cádiz to Santa Cruz weekly. You can also sail to Tenerife from any other Canary Island and there is a hydrofoil service to and from Gran Canaria which takes 80 minutes.
There is a passenger only hydrofoil service from Los Cristianos to San Sebastián on La Gomera (which takes 35 minutes) and two shipping lines (Ferry Gomera and Trasmediterránea) which run regular car and passenger ferries on the same route with a journey time of around 90 minutes.

Entry Formalities

EU citizens, including British citizens, require a passport but do not require a visa whatever the length and purpose of their visit. Holders of US and Canadian passports only require a visa for visits exceeding 90 days.

Camping

Tenerife has just one official site; the well-equipped Nauta Camping/Caravanning at Cañada Blanca, Las Galletas (tel: 78 51 18) with space for 700 people. If you do see backpackers on southern Tenerife it is likely they are off to La Gomera – probably to the Valle Gran Rey, which is particularly popular with campers and those in search of an alternative lifestyle. There is also just one designated site on La Gomera, at Caseiro de

Cedro on the edge of the Parque Nacional de Garajonay. This is administered by the island government office and if you wish to camp here you should contact the office in San Sebastián, Carretera General del Sur 20 (tel: 87 01 05). Camping within the national parks is strictly forbidden on La Gomera and on Tenerife. Climbers and keen walkers in the Parque Nacional del Teide may apply to use the spartan mountain refuge at Altavista (contact ICONA, Santa Cruz, Tenerife, tel: 28 35 58).

Car Rental

Car rental on Tenerife is very cheap compared with the rest of Europe.

Reliable and competitively priced local firms include Top-Car Reisen, with airport offices at Tenerife South/Reina Sofía (tel: 77 32 06) and Tenerife North/Los Rodeos (tel: 26 22 02). Alternatively if you wish to book from the UK, Europe's largest car-hire brokers, Holiday Autos have a lowest pre-booked price guarantee (tel: 0990 300400).

All British, European, American and Australian driving licences are valid. An International Driving Permit is not necessary.

Crime

Theft from cars is the most common form of crime against tourists on the islands. Never leave anything of value on show in your car and try to avoid parking in secluded places.

The Anaga mountains are wonderful walking territory

Hotels usually have a safe for hire, though staff are invariably very honest and break-ins are rare. Apartments are less easy to police so be on your guard. If you are a victim of robbery and wish to make a claim against your insurance policy, you must report the incident to the local police who will give you a copy of your statement for this purpose.

Customs Regulations

There are no limits on the amounts of alcohol and tobacco that can be brought onto the islands, but the prices of these products are so low in the Canaries that it is usually a pointless exercise to do so. Despite the islands' EU status, the restricted export duty-free limits on drinks, tobacco, perfumes, etc, still apply: 200 cigarettes or 100 cigarillos or 250g tobacco or 50 cigars; 1 litre of spirits over 22 per cent proof or 2 litres of fortified or sparkling wine, plus 2 litres of still wine: 60cc perfume or 250cc toilet water; £32 worth of gifts per person, but not more than 50 litres of beer or 25 cigarette lighters. This arrangement is due to change soon to the more relaxed EU limits.

Disabilities see Visitors with Disabilities

Driving

It is possible to take your own car to the islands via mainland Spain (see **Arriving by Sea**, page 113) but as the Canary Islands have very reasonable car hire rates, it is rarely worth

the effort. Contact your motoring organisation for further advice.

Driving Conditions

The standard of roads is high, with many newly built and very smoothly surfaced. Motorway runs along part of the north coast and down the east coast, from Puerto de la Cruz to Playa de las Américas. The first stretch, to Santa Cruz, is known as the Autopista del Norte (north), and thereafter it is called the Autopista del Sur (south). You will probably encounter traffic jams in Playa de las Américas, Puerto de la Cruz and Santa Cruz. The lack of parking and fiendish one-way systems also make driving something of a challenge in these towns. Never stop on narrow, winding mountain roads to enjoy the view, unless you can safely pull off the road. *Miradores* (lookout points) are placed every few kilometres specifically for this purpose.

Parking

In areas marked with blue lines you must buy a parking ticket between 09.00–14.00hrs and 16.00–20.00hrs. If you forget or exceed your time and get a fine notice you can pay this on the spot. Press the button marked *anulación de denuncia*, insert 150 pesetas, then enclose this ticket with the fine and put it in the box below the machine.

Petrol

Petrol is quite expensive and it's best to carry cash, as not all petrol stations accept credit cards. These are relatively numerous along the main roads with 24-hour opening in the larger resorts and towns. Don't drive into the mountains on an empty tank. There are few if any filling stations and those steep winding roads are thirsty work.

Rules and Regulations

The same rules of the road apply as in mainland Europe – drive on the right, overtake on the left and give way to traffic approaching from the right. Use of seat belts is compulsory, except in towns. Children under 10 must travel in the back seat.

Electricity

The current is 220 volts AC and sockets take the circular two-pin continental-style plug, so you will need an adaptor for appliances brought from the UK. You may find 110 volts supply, but this is rare. Ask if in doubt. Power cuts are not infrequent, so pack a torch.

Embassies and Consulates

Ireland: (consulate) Santa Cruz, Tenerife (tel: 24 56 71); (embassy) Madrid (tel: 01-576 35 00).
United Kingdom: (consulate) Plaza de Weyler, 8, Santa Cruz, Tenerife (tel: 28 68 63); (embassy) Madrid (tel: 01-319 02 00).

Emergency Telephone Number

Police/Fire/Ambulance: 091

Health

No vaccinations are necessary for a visit to the Canary Islands. EU citizens can obtain a refund of most medical costs by using form E111 (available from post offices and Health and/or Social Security offices in your own country). If you don't take this along, you can still claim back later (remember to keep all receipts). Personal travel insurance is still advisable. The most common complaints are stomach upsets, caused by a sudden change of diet, and too much sun. Break yourself in gradually to sunbathing and always use suntan lotions and blocks. Remember children are particularly vulnerable. There are many English-speaking dentists and doctors throughout the islands. Ask your hotel or tourist information office for the nearest one or see the list in the *Tenerife Holiday Gazette*.

Holidays

Fixed Dates
1 January – Año Nuevo (New Year's Day)
6 January – Los Reyes (Epiphany)
2 February – La Candelaria (Candlemas)
1 May – Día del Trabajo (Labour Day)
25 July – Santiago (St James's Day)
15 August – Asunción (Assumption)
12 October – Día de la Hispanidad (Discovery of America/Colombus Day)
1 November – Todos los Santos (All Saints' Day)
6 December – Día de la Constitución (Constitution Day)
25 December – Navidad (Christmas Day)

Movable Feasts
Jueves Santo (Maundy Thursday)

Viernes Santo (Good Friday)
Pascua (Easter Sunday)
Lunes de Pascua (Easter
Monday)
Corpus Christi – May/June
Concepción (Conception) –
usually 8 December.

In addition to these, there are
several *patronales* (local patron
saint feast days), when there will
be processions and fireworks.

Lost Property

Lost property offices are few and
far between. Ask the tourist office
where to go locally. Report lost
valuables to the **Policía
Municipal** or **Guardia Civil** and
obtain a form for your own
holiday insurance purposes.

Media

The free *Tenerife Holiday
Gazette* comes out monthly and
is a useful source of listings and
general information. Pick up a
copy from the tourist office.
Island Connections covers all the
islands and is worth buying,
available from newsagents in
the tourist areas. The only other
English-language printed media
is the lamentable *Island Sun*
newspaper, which covers all the
Canary Islands.
Waves FM broadcasts in English
to Tenerife and La Gomera on
96.8FM. News is on the hour and
the quality of programmes,
mostly music, is high. BBC
World Service and the Voice of
America can be picked up on
short wave.
Many hotels and some bars
have a bewildering selection of
cable and satellite TV channels.
For a full listing see *Island
Connections*.

*Procession at Icod de los Vinos –
one of the island's many feast days*

In the tourist resorts of the
south, English newspapers are
available on the day of
publication, while European
papers and the *International
Herald Tribune* and *The
Guardian* (international edition)
can arrive the same day, almost
everywhere.

Money Matters

The Spanish *peseta* (pta) is the
unit of currency in circulation
throughout the islands.
Banks are open Monday to
Friday 09.00–14.00hrs and
Saturdays 09.00–13.00hrs
(closed on Saturdays from
1 June to 31 October). A
commission is always charged

DIRECTORY

The Iglesia de Santa Catalina at Tacoronte belies its somewhat dull exterior

for changing money (often hefty, so exchange large amounts if possible) and you will need your passport. Outside banking hours many travel agents and various bureaux de change (look for the *cambio* sign) will exchange money, often at competitive rates.

Do *not* change money at tourist shops. Even if the rates on display seem attractive the deductions which they conveniently omit to display will cost you dearly. Hotels will also change money, but at a low rate. Credit card cash dispensers are common in Santa Cruz and the major tourist resorts.

Credit Cards

Most hotels, many restaurants, shops and all car rental firms accept major credit cards. Not all petrol stations do.

Opening Times

Offices

Usually Monday to Friday 09.00–13.00hrs and 15.00–19.00hrs; Saturday 09.00–13.00hrs.

Shops

Traditional hours are Monday to Friday 09.00–13.00hrs and 16.00–20.00hrs; Saturday 09.00–13.00hrs. In the main tourist resorts shops may open all day seven days a week. Museum opening hours vary; consult individual entries. Church hours are also unpredictable. Where hours are not given for individual entries, morning or evening service times will usually find them open.

Pharmacies

Open Monday to Friday 09.00–13.00hrs and 16.00–20.00hrs; Saturday 09.00–13.00hrs. Minor ailments can usually be treated at the pharmacy (*farmacia*), signposted by a green cross. At least one pharmacy per town or area stays open after hours (*farmacia de guardia*). Its location is posted in the window of all the other pharmacies (also available from the tourist office and local newspaper).

Places of Worship

Catholic Mass is celebrated in various languages in all the major resorts, including English services in the parish church of Our Lady of Guadalupe in Playa de las Américas (behind the tax office building), and in Our Lady of Mount Carmel in Los Cristianos.

Anglican services are held in the Anglican church at Taoro Park, Puerto de la Cruz, and in the San Eugenio church in the Pueblo Canario in Playa de las Américas.

Evangelical services take place at Hotel Andreas, Los Cristianos and the Evangelical Church on Calle Iriarte, Puerto de la Cruz. Ask the tourist office, see the local newspapers, *Tenerife Holiday Gazette*, or look on church noticeboards for details.

Police

Police responsibilities are split three ways on the islands. The *Policía Municipal* (blue uniform) direct traffic and have other municipal duties; the *Policía Nacional* (brown uniform) deal with crime in the towns; the *Guardia Civil* (pea-green uniform) deal with crime and patrol the highways in rural areas.

In an emergency tel: 091.

Post Offices

Post offices (*Correos*) are open Monday to Friday 09.00–14.00hrs and Saturdays 09.00–13.00hrs. There are no telephones in post offices. Stamps (*sellos* or *timbres*) can also be bought at tobacconists and most shops which sell postcards.

Postboxes are painted yellow. Use the slot marked *extranjeros* (foreign) for post home.

Public Transport

Buses

The service run by TITSA, is extensive, cheap, fast and reliable. If you intend travelling a lot on buses, consider buying a *bono* (voucher) which for around 2,000 pesetas entitles you to buy tickets at a 25 per cent discount. The most popular routes and fares are listed in the *Tenerife Holiday Gazette*.

Taxis

These are recognisable by a green light in the windscreen or on a white roof and an official plate with the letters SP, standing for *servicio público* (public service). The light shows *libre* (free) when they are available for hire. For short trips within tourist areas many cabbies won't bother to put their meters on, though you will rarely be cheated. Boards by the main taxi ranks display fixed prices between the most popular destinations and sample fares are also listed in the *Tenerife Holiday Gazette*.

A cab here is still good value by north European standards. For longer distances confirm the price, or rate, before you start.

Senior Citizens

The elderly are well catered for in many hotels on Tenerife, with a specific style of holiday and long-stay discounts. However, note that getting around is not always easy for holiday-makers who are infirm or need a wheelchair (see **Visitors with Disabilities**, page 122).

Student and Youth Travel

With the exception of Valle Gran Rey on La Gomera, Tenerife does not attract the backpacking youngsters seen on many other holiday islands worldwide. There are no youth hostels. (See **Camping**, page 114.)

Telephones

You can now make international calls from virtually any phone on the islands. The best way to phone home is from a *telefónica* cabin, which comprises metered booths where you pay after your call. This is not much more expensive than a street phone and is much less draughty, less noisy and you don't need mountains of change to hand. Be aware that the LED indicator above your phone is *not* the amount in pesetas you are spending, but the unit charge. *Telefónicas* are generally in central locations and open late.

The easiest way to squander money phoning home is by using the telephone in your hotel room, as most hotels levy a costly surcharge.

Codes to Tenerife

The code for Tenerife and La Gomera is **922**. When you are calling from outside the Canaries however, drop the 9, ie, from abroad dial 00-34-22 then the number.

Locals taking life easy in Santa Cruz

You can phone home from anywhere on Tenerife

different start/end dates to summer time.

Tipping
On Tenerife most hotels and some restaurant bills include a service charge. A small tip, however, (around 10 per cent) for a well-served meal, a friendly taxi driver, or hotel staff who have been particularly helpful, will be appreciated. Don't forget to leave the hotel maid something too.

Toilets
Public toilets are very rare and recommendable public toilets rarer still. In order of preference use those in hotels, restaurants and bars. Do buy a drink in the latter as a matter of courtesy. There are several terms for toilets: *servicios, aseos, WC, retretes.* The doors are usually marked *Señoras* (ladies) and *Caballeros* (gentlemen) or will use a familiar pictogram.

Codes from Tenerife
For international calls, dial 07, wait for the tone to indicate that you have a line, then dial your country code (Australia 61, Canada and the USA 1, Ireland 353, UK 44), followed by the local code minus the first 0 (if there is one), then the number.

Time
The Canaries maintain Greenwich Mean Time in the winter, which is one hour behind most European countries and in line with the UK. The clocks go forward one hour in summer time, as does everyone else, so maintaining the difference.

The Canaries are 5 hours ahead of US Eastern Standard Time, and 8 hours ahead of Pacific Time. Johannesburg is ahead by one hour, Australia by 10 hours and New Zealand by 12 hours. Note that there are two brief periods of one-hour difference to this rule (in late September and late March) owing to

Tourist Offices
United Kingdom
Spanish Tourist Office: 57–8 St James's Street, London SW1A 1LD, tel: 0171 499 0901. (Relocating during 1997.)

US
Tourist Office of Spain, 665 Fifth Avenue, New York, NY 10022, tel: 212/759 8822.

Canada
Tourist Office of Spain, 102 Bloor Street West, 14th Floor, Toronto, Ontario M5S 1M8, tel: 416/961 3131.

The harbour at Los Cristianos is busy with the local fishing fleet as well as visiting pleasure craft

Tenerife
Garachico: Artesanía El Limonero, opposite Castillo San Miguel on the seafront (tel: 13 34 34).
Playa de las Américas: in front of Centro Commercial City Center (tel: 79 76 68).
Puerto de la Cruz: Plaza de la Iglesia 3 (tel: 38 60 00).
Santa Cruz de Tenerife: Palacio Insular, Plaza de España (tel: 60 55 92).

La Gomera
San Sebastián de la Gomera: Pozo de la Aguada, Calle del Medio (tel: 14 01 47).

Visitors with Disabilities
The most wheelchair-friendly part of Tenerife is the south. Los Cristianos has a good reputation for its facilities, with ramps provided throughout the town. The Mar y Sol resort has been purpose-built for holiday-makers with disabilities. For direct information, tel: 79 54 73; for information from the UK contact ATS Travel, tel: 01708 863198. Mar y Sol also have a comprehensive range of disability appliances for hire. Away from the new resorts general facilities are poor to non-existent. There are very few adapted toilets, no adapted public transport facilities nor adapted hire cars (even automatics are rare). Kerbs are generally high, often blocked by parked cars, there are cobbled streets in the older towns, and the hilly nature of the terrain means pushers will have to work hard. There are wheelchair facilities at both airports.
The Spanish association for travellers with disabilities is Federation ECOM, Gran Vía de les Corts Catalanes 562 prat.2, 08011 Barcelona, tel: 03-451 5550. Travellers from the United Kingdom should contact the Holiday Care Service for fact sheets on Tenerife and for any general advice: 2nd Floor, Imperial Building, Victoria Road, Horley, Surrey, RH6 7PZ, tel: 01293 774535.

LANGUAGE

The Canary Islanders speak Spanish and the only major difference from the mainland is that the letters c and z are pronounced softly, instead of lisped with a 'th' sound.

There are a few indigenous words still in use, the most notable: *papa(s)* for potato(es) and *guagua* (pronounced 'wah-wah') for bus.

Pronunciation
Vowels

a is a short 'ah' sound in *gracias* (thank you).

e is a cross between the short English e (as in get) and the long English a (as in grace), eg *de* (of/from) is pronounced 'day' but in a clipped way.

i is a long 'ee' sound as in *sí* (yes) pronounced 'see'.

u is like 'oo' in boot eg *una* (one).

Consonants

c is soft before e and before i (eg Barcelona) but hard at any other time.

g at the start of a word is a hard sound (as in get). In the middle of a word however it is like the throaty ch as in the Scottish loch, eg *urgencia* (emergency) is pronounced 'ooor-chensee-ah'. In *agua* (water) it is hardly pronounced at all ('ah-kwa').

h is always silent.

j is also pronounced like the ch in loch, eg *jamón* (ham) is pronounced 'ch-amon'.

ll is like 'll' in million eg *lleno* (full) is pronounced 'lyay-no'.

ñ is like 'ni' in onion, eg *España* (Spain) pronounced 'ay-spanya'.

qu is like k in key, eg *cuánto?* (how much?) is pronounced 'kwan-toe'.

r is rolled, rr is rolled even harder.

v is like b in bottle, eg *vino* (wine) is pronounced 'bee-no'.

x is like s, eg *excelente* (excellent) is pronounced 'ess-say-len-tay'

Useful words and phrases

yes/no sí/no
hello hola
good morning buenos días
good afternoon buenas tardes
goodnight buenas noches
goodbye adiós
see you later hasta luego
please por favor
thank you gracias
you're welcome de nada
sir, madame, miss señor, señora, señorita
excuse me perdóneme,
sorry! ¡lo siento!
today hoy
tomorrow mañana
yesterday ayer
last night anoche
tonight esta noche
how are you? ¿cómo está?
very well/good muy bien/vale
can you help please? ¿me podría ayudar por favor?
I am English soy inglés
I am sorry, but I don't speak Spanish lo siento, pero no hablo español
do you speak English? ¿habla inglés?
is there someone who speaks...? hay alguien que hable...?
I don't understand no comprendo
what is your name? ¿cómo te llamas?
my name is... minombre es.../me llamo...

LANGUAGE

what do you call…? ¿cómo se llama…?
what time is it? ¿qué hora es?
can I get past? ¿podría pasar?
can you…? ¿puede usted/puedes…?
how much is…? ¿cuánto vale/cuesta…?
is there?/there is… ¿hay?/hay…
I would like… quiero/quisiera…
where is …? ¿dónde está…?
what/when qué/cuándo
why/how por qué/cómo
near/far cerca/lejos
here/there aquí/ahí
old/new viejo/nuevo
cheap/expensive barato/caro
open/closed abierto/cerrado
right/left derecho/izquierdo
for, to por/para, a/para
large/small grande/pequeño

more/less más/menos
the key la llave
bathroom/toilet (cuarto de) baño/servicio
the bill la cuenta
ticket(s) billete(s)
stamp(s) sello(s)
bus station estación de guagua
church iglesia

Days of the Week
Monday lunes
Tuesday martes
Wednesday miercoles
Thursday jueves
Friday viernes
Saturday sábado
Sunday domingo

Local art along the Paseo de San Telmo, Puerto de la Cruz

INDEX

INDEX/ACKNOWLEDGEMENTS

Acknowledgements
The Automobile Association wishes to thank the following photographers
and libraries for their assistance in the preparation of this book:

MARY EVANS PICTURE LIBRARY 15
INTERNATIONAL PHOTOBANK 48/9
PAUL MURPHY 91
NATURE PHOTOGRAPHERS LTD 94 (B Burbidge), 96 (P R Sterry),
97 (B Burbidge), 98 (M Bolton)
PICTURES COLOUR LIBRARY 4, 118
SPECTRUM COLOUR LIBRARY 117, 122, 124

The remaining photographs are held in the Association's own library
(© AA PHOTO LIBRARY) and were taken by Rob Moore, pages 9, 12, 18, 22,
23, 26, 28, 32, 34, 41, 42, 47, 56, 63, 64, 65, 70, 71, 72, 75, 77, 102, 108, 109,
112 and Clive Sawyer, cover and pages 7, 8, 10, 11, 24, 25, 29, 30, 35, 37, 39,
45, 46, 50, 51, 53, 54/5, 57, 58/9, 61, 62, 67, 68, 73, 76, 78/9, 80, 81, 82, 83, 86,
87, 88, 89, 90, 92/3, 100, 101, 103, 104, 106, 110/11, 111, 114, 120, 121.

Author's Acknowledgements
The author would like to thank the following for their kind help and hospitality:
Sr Rafael Cabral of Top-Car Reisen; the management of the Hotel Jardín
Tecina, La Gomera; and the staff of the Tenerife Tourist Office, Santa Cruz
de Tenerife.

Contributors
Copy editor: Hilary Hughes   **Verifier**: Teresa Fisher
Designer: The Company of Designers   **Indexer**: Marie Lorimer